THE SHAKESPEARE PLAYS

HENRY IV Part 2

D1509130

THE SHAKESPEARE PLAYS

THE SHAKESPEARE PLAYS

Literary Consultant: John Wilders

Henry IV Part 2

MAYFLOWER BOOKS
NEW YORK

CONTENTS

PREFACE

Cedric Messina

The BBC Television Shakespeare moves into its second year with productions of *Henry IV Part 1*, *Henry IV Part 2*, *Henry V*, *The Tempest*, *Twelfth Night* and *Hamlet*. The plan is to present the thirty-seven plays in groups of six a year for six years, with one odd man out. The productions have now been sold for showing throughout the world, thus fulfilling the public broadcasting ideal behind the series – to make them available to audiences who would have no other access to Shakespeare. Transmissions of the first six plays (*Romeo and Juliet*, *Richard II*, *As You Like It*, *Julius Caesar*, *Measure for Measure* and *Henry VIII*) have already been completed in many countries, notably the USA, Canada and Australia. Japan, Mexico, Hungary, Rumania, Hong Kong, Taiwan, France and many others have bought the plays, but in many cases have not yet finally decided whether they should be dubbed or subtitled. Many of the languages involved have splendid translations of some of the major plays, but only a few have excellent versions of the whole canon.

Thirty-six of the plays were published in the First Folio of 1623, exactly half of which had never been published before. (The thirty-seventh is *Pericles, Prince of Tyre*, first published in the Quarto of 1609.) *Henry IV Part 2* was first published in Quarto form in 1600, with the title '*The Second part of Henrie the fourth, continuing to his death, and coronation of Henrie the fift. With the humours of Sir John Falstaffe, and swaggering Pistoll. As it hath been sundrie times publikely acted by the right honourable, the Lord Chamberlaine his servants*'. The production was recorded at the BBC Television Centre at White City, London, in April 1979.

The television production of *2 Henry IV* begins, as does *Part 1*, with a flashback, showing the seizure of the anointed King Richard II's crown by Bolingbroke, now King Henry IV, and the subsequent murder in Pomfret Castle of Richard – an event which is to haunt Henry to the moment of his death. Like the curse on the House of Atreus in Aeschylus' great trilogy *The Oresteia*, this murder of an anointed king is to cast its shadow over Shakespeare's trilogy. And indeed over the *Henry VI* plays, and in *Richard III* Rivers at Pomfret Castle recalls the murder of Richard II years after the event.

There are not as many scenes of court life and high politics as in Part 1, and the play introduces two great new characters in the low life of Cheapside – Doll Tearsheet, the sluttish companion of Mistress Quickly, and Pistol, the ultimate military swaggerer. The love scene between Doll Tearsheet (played by Frances Cuka) and Anthony Quayle's Falstaff, overheard by Hal and Poins disguised as musicians, is one of the many delights of the play. Although much of the action passes in the Boar's Head tavern – the same sets as in the production of *1 Henry IV* – it is when Falstaff and his entourage move to Gloucestershire that the full, fine comic writing of Shakespeare surely makes Falstaff one of his greatest creations. It was the success of Falstaff in Part 1 that made Shakespeare sit down almost immediately and write this sequel. Justice Shallow and his friends and servants provide the backdrop to the comic yokels, the puns, the wanderings of Shallow, and the autumnal regrets of things long since past, brutally exploded by Pistol, whose arrival with the news of the death of King Henry makes Falstaff exult at the thought of the honours he will now receive at the hands of his beloved Prince Hal, now King. The whole group rush to London in high expectation, to be next seen on the coronation day of King Henry V.

The King, Hal and his brothers feature in the play, and like all families, they have their good and their bad members. Prince John, in his dealings with the usurpers in Yorkshire's Gaultree Forest, is treacherous and dishonest. But the King and his heir are the protagonists of the plan, and in a series of scenes, closely shot in this production, Jon Finch and David Gwillim give depth and understanding to their ambiguous relationship. When Henry feels that he is dying and wishes to see Hal, his three brothers are unable to keep the news from him that Hal is carousing with his usual companions. Left alone, the king falls into a coma, the crown beside him. Hal enters the dimly-let room and, believing the king to be dead, picks up the crown, places it on his head, and moves into another room. Television heightens the scene with its close-up of the king's awakening and realising that his crown has disappeared. He is shattered when he finds that Hal has already taken it, and has, indeed, tried it on. In one of the greatest father and son scenes ever written by Shakespeare, the two actors explore the situation which is resolved by the death of Henry. But the shadow of Richard II falls across their death-bed reconciliation, and the legality of his having the crown at all is to plague Hal even on the field of Agincourt the night before the battle.

On Henry V's coronation day one of the most perplexing scenes in all of Shakespeare's works is enacted, when from the throng Falstaff with great gusto and familiarity salutes the king. He is rebuffed, denied access to the King's person, and finally sent off to prison for a while. This extraordinary volte-face and cruel act is puzzling to many modern audiences, but to Elizabethans it seemed natural that the king should protect his crown and reputation, as their current sovereign Elizabeth had discarded Essex when he threatened not only the monarch and the crown, but its very reputation. But as the king David Gwillim, his hair now cut in the Henry V fashion, gives us a taste of what he is to become as Henry V, and Anthony Quayle's Falstaff leaves the trilogy with tears streaming down his face, his rejection stunning him and his dreams of glory all faded away.

It was decided to publish the plays, using the Peter Alexander edition, the same text as used in the production of the plays, and one very widely used in the academic world. But these texts with their theatrical divisions into scenes and acts are supplemented with their television equivalents. In other words we are also publishing the television scripts on which the production was based. There are colour and black and white photographs of the production, a general introduction to the play by Dr John Wilders and an article by Henry Fenwick which includes interviews with the actors, directors, designers and costume designers, giving their reactions to the special problems their contributions encountered in the transfer of the plays to the screen. The volumes include a newly-compiled glossary and a complete cast list of the performers, including the names of the technicians, costume designers and scenic designers responsible for the play.

INTRODUCTION TO
HENRY IV PART 2

John Wilders

In certain fairly obvious ways the Second Part of *Henry IV* resembles the First Part. In the earlier of the two plays Prince Hal separates himself from his apparently frivolous association with Falstaff, makes a pledge to the King that he will take on his public responsibilities, demonstrates his loyalty by taking part in the Battle of Shrewsbury and, in the final moments, stands victorious over the body of the rebel leader and his own rival, Hotspur. In *Part 2* Hal is, for a second time, thought by the King to be neglecting his duty and to be likely, on his accession to the throne, to become an irresponsible ruler, incapable of winning the respect of his people. Towards the end of the play, however, the Prince again shows his good intentions by entrusting the law to the authority of the Lord Chief Justice and displays his final separation from Falstaff by banishing the latter from his company and announcing that he is no longer the profligate he once appeared to be. Whereas in *Part 1* Hal exhibited his military virtues and loyalty in battle, so in *Part 2* he manifests his civic virtues, his reverence for the law. And as the defeat of Hotspur forms the climax and conclusion of the earlier play, so the rejection of Falstaff completes the latter.

The action of *2 Henry IV* is again distributed mostly between three locations: Falstaff continues to occupy the tavern, the King meditates on his own past in the isolation of the palace, and the rebels are again confronted and overcome on the battlefield, though this time without a struggle. Several of the minor characters also reappear: Mistress Quickly, Bardolph, Lady Percy, and Northumberland, whose career we can follow from his first appearance at the court of Richard II to his defeat in Yorkshire reported in this play. The inclusion of these same characters conveys to us the sense of the continuing movement of history and, more importantly, makes us realise how they, and circumstances, have changed.

One striking change is the absence from 2 *Henry IV* of Hotspur. His inspired leadership and his enjoyment of the challenge of war coloured the first phase of the rebellion with an attractive vitality, an exciting recklessness. He was motivated not simply by contempt for the monarch whom his family had helped into power but by the pursuit of military glory for its own sake. With his death the rebels have no such heroic ideal to support them; they are deprived of a leader of any stature and seem uncertain of their own motives. Northumberland, maddened with grief at the death of his son, cries out for slaughter as a means of revenging himself upon the world. Archbishop Scroop, who has replaced Hotspur at the head of the rebellion, believes the nation is sick and takes upon himself the responsibility of purging it by insurrection; his ally, Lord Bardolph, appears to revolt merely in response to the earlier defeat at Shrewsbury. They are, we are told, accompanied by an army of commoners as disenchanted with Henry IV as they had been with Richard II. Such motives are not inspiring nor even respectable. The revolution is apparently failing for want of conviction.

The vitality has also gone out of Falstaff. In *Part 1*, although obviously irresponsible, a liar and a cheat, he was, nevertheless, capable of transforming his weaknesses into assets by the single-minded enthusiasm with which he indulged them. In *Part 2*, far from commanding the tavern by the largeness of his personality, he is actually dominated for a time by the bizarre, disreputable Pistol, whose misquotations from plays once fashionable but now outmoded suggest that he has lost touch with the times. Wearied by Pistol's continual ranting, Falstaff pathetically, and uncharacteristically, asks for quiet.

Another reason why Falstaff appears tarnished is the almost total absence from the tavern of Prince Hal. Among his associates Hal was his only equal in initiative, vitality and quickness of wit; the one relied upon and inspired the other. In the Second Part they are together only twice: once in the tavern, and once during Hal's progress from his coronation when he meets his former companion for the last time and disowns him. When the Prince, with some reluctance, pays his last visit to the Boar's Head, in a scene placed at exactly the same point (Act II Scene iv) as the great tavern scene in *Part 1*, it is obvious that he has outgrown Falstaff. The two no longer talk to each other as equals. Hal accuses Falstaff of slandering him to the Hostess:

You whoreson candle-mine, you, how vilely did you speak of

me even now before this honest, virtuous, civil gentlewoman!

But Falstaff no longer has the wit to take up this challenge. His retort is feebly ingratiating:

> No, no, no; not so; I did not think thou wast within hearing . . . No abuse, Hal, o' mine honour; no abuse . . . No abuse, Ned, i' th' world; honest Ned, none. I disprais'd him before the wicked – that the wicked might not fall in love with thee; in which doing, I have done the part of a careful friend and a true subject.

He struggles ineffectually to creep into the favour of the heir apparent. Falstaff had always been a boaster but his former claims to courage, loyalty, honesty and good looks were so outrageous that they amounted to self-parody, designed to be only half believed. In the Second Part he is smug. His tedious, self-glorifying monologues are delivered not to the Prince but to his newly-acquired page. They might as well be delivered into vacancy. Hal's absence from the tavern makes Falstaff appear shrunk and serves as a warning to the audience that the Prince has dissociated himself from the common people and is advancing towards that solitary eminence which his father is about to relinquish. It is a warning which Falstaff does not heed.

Such criticisms as Falstaff receives are not the affectionate insults he formerly suffered from Hal but the honest, disinterested truth spoken by the Lord Chief Justice. He tries to draw the latter into the game of self-deception he had confidently played with Hal:

> You that are old consider not the capacities of us that are young; you do measure the heat of our livers with the bitterness of your galls; and we that are in the vaward of our youth, I must confess, are wags too.

The Lord Chief Justice is not enchanted but treats Falstaff's pretensions to youth with derision:

> Do you set down your name in the scroll of youth, that are written down old with all the characters of age? Have you not a moist eye, a dry hand, a yellow cheek, a white beard, a decreasing leg, an increasing belly? Is not your voice broken, your wind short, your chin double, your wit single, and every part about you blasted with antiquity? And will you yet call yourself young? Fie, fie, fie, Sir John!

In Part One the Prince had called him, among other things, a 'bed-presser', but the audience was denied the spectacle of Falstaff actually pressing a bed. In the Second Part he appears in the company of a new character, Doll Tearsheet, a whore, whom he accuses of spreading syphilis. His body is consumed with the pox as his purse is with extravagance and both diseases are incurable. In one moment of truth he admits, 'I am old'.

Most of the time, however, he continues to behave as though neither he nor circumstances have changed, assured of his own charms, confident that the Prince will, on his accession, long to see him and will make him great. Because the audience knows otherwise and sees through his delusions they regard his optimism as pathetic. The irony with which Shakespeare induces us to view Falstaff's hopes becomes extreme when, knowing that the Prince has already entrusted the law to the Lord Chief Justice, we observe Falstaff rushing eagerly to London in the belief that the young King is sick for him:

> Let us take any man's horses: the laws of England are at my commandment. Blessed are they that have been my friends; and woe to my Lord Chief Justice!

Henry V's rejection of Falstaff comes as no surprise to us. Yet Falstaff still refuses to accept the truth: he disappears from Hal's life protesting that he will be 'sent for soon at night'.

The belief that nothing has changed also afflicts another new character, Justice Shallow, and we can see why. The regular, seasonal life of his farm in Gloucestershire has repeated itself annually without alteration. We learn from his rambling conversations with his cousin Silence and his servant Davy that bullocks are still sold at Stamford fair, that his land will again be sown with red wheat and that the smith continues to make plough irons and new links for the bucket. Shallow's neighbours have extraordinary rural names such as William Visor of Woncot and Clement Perkes o' th' Hill. Their association with specific places in Gloucestershire conveys the impression that their families have lived there for generations (and, indeed, the scholars have discovered that the Visors actually did live at Woodmancote, or 'Woncot', not far from Berkeley Castle where Richard II had arrived on his return from Ireland). But as the seasonal processes of nature have recurred, Robert Shallow has grown old and, living in this rural backwater, he keeps himself alive with distorted recollections of his youth:

I was once of Clement's Inn; where I think they will talk of mad Shallow yet. . . . There was I, and little John Doit of Staffordshire, and black George Barnes, and Francis Pickbone, and Will Squele a Cotsole man – you had not four such swingebucklers in all the Inns o' Court again. And I may say to you we knew where the bona-robas were, and had the best of them all at commandment. . . . Jesu, Jesu, the mad days that I have spent!

As the ageing Falstaff lives in hopes of a spectacular future, so Shallow cheers himself with the recollection of a past which never existed: 'Lord, Lord', says Falstaff, 'how subject we old men are to this vice of lying!'

In no other play does Shakespeare convey so fully and so intimately the effects of age. They show themselves in the dying King's anxieties for the future of his people, in Lady Percy's memories of the dead Hotspur, in Shallow's illogical, bemused conversations, and the state of Falstaff's urine. Whereas the distinctive quality of Shakespeare's writing in Part One (as I suggested in my Introduction to that play) is its expansive vitality, the dialogue of Part Two conveys a sense of exhaustion:

King Henry. Then you perceive the body of our kingdom
How foul it is; what rank diseases grow,
And with what danger, near the heart of it.

Archbishop. We are all diseas'd
And with our surfeiting and wanton hours
Have brought ourselves into a burning fever,
And we must bleed for it.

Lord Chief Justice to Falstaff. You are as a candle, the better part burnt out.

Shallow. Is old Double of your town living yet?
Silence. Dead, sir.

The sense of disintegration, sickness and mortality felt by so many of the characters is a manifestation of the more fundamental process of change itself which, as it propels King Henry, Falstaff and Shallow towards death and obscurity, brings Prince Hal towards power.

The world of 2 *Henry IV* is an unstable, insecure one where events turn out contrary to the expectations of the characters: the first scene opens with the arrival of three successive messengers

14

carrying conflicting news of victory and defeat; Falstaff reaches Westminster 'stained with travel', 'sweating with desire' to see the new King, only to be brushed aside, rejected; the rebels, believing they have been offered a fair peace, disband their soldiers and are promptly escorted to the executioner's block; the Prince, thinking his father dead, takes up the crown and resolves to wear it with honour, only to discover that the King is still alive; and Henry, imagining that he will die as a pilgrim in Jerusalem, ends his life in a room in the palace of that name. The play is introduced by a Prologue spoken by the allegorical figure of Rumour whose nature it is to spread 'surmises, jealousies [or suspicions], conjectures' and it is on false surmises that King Henry, Falstaff, Shallow and the rebels build their lives. Only the Prince foresees the future correctly and that is because he has the power and ability to control it.

A bewildered weariness with the unpredictability of life, a conviction that the only certainty is change itself, is powerfully expressed in a great speech by the King whose own troubled experience has given him good reason to believe it:

O God! that one might read the book of fate,
And see the revolution of the times
Make mountains level, and the continent,
Weary of solid firmness, melt itself
Into the sea; and other times to see
The beachy girdle of the ocean
Too wide for Neptune's hips; how chances mock,
And changes fill the cup of alteration
With divers liquors! O, if this were seen,
The happiest youth, viewing his progress through,
What perils past, what crosses to ensue,
Would shut the book and sit him down and die.

For Henry, it seems, the only thing which makes the instability of history tolerable is our customary ignorance of it.

There is, however, a secure foundation on which a king can rest his authority and that is the man-made principles of justice and the law. If we trace the civil wars which plagued Henry IV back to their origins, we can find them in Richard II's disregard for the law in seizing the estates which belonged by right to Bolingbroke, and in Bolingbroke's consequent usurpation of the throne which was, of course, legally Richard's. To break the laws of property and inheritance is easy. They have only as much efficacy as men choose to put in them. But without them nations are in danger of becoming barbarians, and that is what the King believes will happen when his apparently lawless son succeeds him:

> For the fifth Harry from curb'd license plucks
> The muzzle of restraint, and the wild dog
> Shall flesh his tooth on every innocent.

When his son actually does become king, however, the rule of justice is assured and this prospect is foreshadowed when he entrusts the guardianship of the law to the character who embodies it. The Lord Chief Justice is not an interesting man. He is not as engaging as the humanly fallible characters such as Falstaff or Shallow, and, significantly, he has no personal name, only a title. He is, however, dependably honest – not a common virtue in this play – and has a loyalty to the law which takes precedence over his obligations to any individual, including the Prince. Just before his coronation, the new King presents him with the 'unstained sword' of justice, with the injunction that he should

> use the same
> With the like bold, just, and impartial spirit
> As you have done 'gainst me.

In acknowledging the Lord Chief Justice as his father, as he calls him, Henry V implicitly disowns the 'father ruffian' Falstaff, who learns shortly afterwards that the laws of England are not at his commandment.

Of all the rulers whose lives Shakespeare dramatised, Henry V was the most successful. The seemingly frivolous, degenerate youth transformed himself into a responsible king and, out of loyalty to him, his subjects became again united. Yet his final action in this play, his dismissal of Falstaff, inevitable though it is, appears at the same time distasteful, and it confirms the uneasiness Hal has aroused in us from his first appearance in Part One. He has never actually encouraged Falstaff's false expectations. He has promised him nothing. On the contrary he has warned him that his banishment will eventually come. Falstaff's dream of power is largely self-induced, one of the fantasies indulged in by several characters in *Henry IV*. Perhaps what is offensive about Hal is his lack of spontaneity, his ability always to calculate exactly what he is doing and to carry out to the letter the plans he makes for himself. This is particularly striking when we compare him with Falstaff, a creature of instinct, even though it is an instinct to deceive or simply survive. And Falstaff never keeps his maudlin resolutions to mend his ways. When Hal relaxes in the tavern he is the heir-apparent playing at relaxation. When, in both parts, he publicly displays his reformation, he has not really reformed because he has never actually been dissolute. He plays these various roles so skilfully that he even convinces his own father. What, then, is the essential Hal, the man who performs his roles with such professionalism? Shakespeare never reveals him. This is not to say that Shakespeare disapproved of him. He believed that Hal had the qualities necessary for a ruler to be successful. He also recognised that successful kings are not the most congenial individuals.

GENEALOGICAL TABLE

This is a simplified table, showing the succession from Edward III to Henry VIII and those characters who are important in *Henry IV, Parts 1 & 2* and *Henry V*. The dates refer to lives and not to reigns.

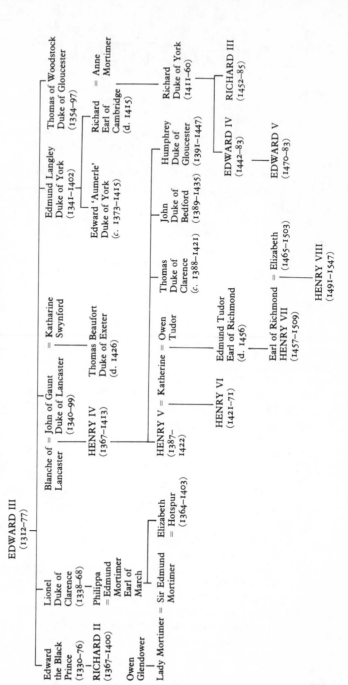

THE PRODUCTION

Henry Fenwick

'I started the three Henry Plays [*1 & 2 Henry IV* and *Henry V*] by having a secret love for Part 2,' says David Giles, the director of the three plays, 'because it is about the state of England. Shakespeare uses the theatre to carry you all over England and to every condition of man from ostlers to the king.' It is also, when viewing the three plays as a continuity, the one which crucially affects the audience's vision of the action and of the 'hero', Prince Hal – later Henry V.

'One of the great advantages of doing the three plays together', says producer Cedric Messina, 'is that the audience can get a much fuller picture of Henry V by seeing his behaviour as Prince Hal. In Part 2 he is feeling things that he thought were foreign to his nature up to that time: he has decided he will take on the responsibility of being heir to the throne, and his rejection of Falstaff is terrible to see. He only appears with Falstaff once in Part 2; roughly speaking, he's no longer with Falstaff and his cronies, he's with his father much more. It's the measure of the actor that you see the transformation going on. His father is getting sicker and sicker and he's aware himself that he's getting nearer and nearer the throne, and he prepares himself all through Part 2. By the end of Part 2, after the rejection of Falstaff, David Gwillim seems a totally different person.'

'Part 2 is very much the death play,' says Giles. 'It's full of images of disease all the time. Falstaff is not nearly so spry, he's still very witty but not nearly as nimble as he was in Part 1. His first line is "What says the doctor to my water?", which means he's worried about his health. He has a wonderful speech about what the inside of a church is like; and when Doll Tearsheet tries to cheer him she says something about his end and he tells her not to talk like a death's head. The whole play is full of death. The king, of course, dies long and lingeringly; we've followed history – or at least some of the chroniclers, who believe he had leprosy. Henry certainly did die of some terrible kind of skin disease, which we play through both parts – he's getting it in Part 1 and he's got it in Part 2.'

For Jon Finch, the sickening and then dying king was far from the usual heroic, rather swashbuckling parts he plays in films. The virile excitement he brought to Bolingbroke in *Richard II* was remarked on, but nobody at that time knew – Finch himself included – that he would be going on to play the man through age and death; though, as Giles points out, our picture of Henry as old is historically incorrect. In fact, the king of Part 1 was about the same age as Finch. The actor had to make a decision, when playing the diseased king, on how far the disease was to take him: 'What happens is Make-up come up to you and say "Do you really want to see this?" and you say, "Yeah, I really want to see it," and they open up a book and start showing you pictures of leprous hands, leprous nose holes, fingers falling off – and the disease gets progressively worse in Part 2. We decided to draw the line at the face – I think it's a little inessential to be very graphic. As long as you know the guy's got leprosy and syphilis, that gives a reason for his collapse and also a measure of sympathy for the character.' He did, however, study the effects of the disease and was able, also, to use the king's weakening condition to good effect in the battle scenes, where sickness helps explain his vulnerability.

'I don't think I've ever worked so closely with designers,' says the director. 'We knew that over the three plays we had this great problem of how to do the battles, and also how to do *Henry V*, which is different stylistically from the other two plays. We talked for hours and hours, and they've been marvellous about coming in to rehearsal to see how it's going. We felt that in Parts 1 and 2 the scenes should be very definitely localised. They're done quite simply and Dennis [Channon] lit them beautifully. We decided exactly what we needed and wanted from each scene and then created sets round it. We also decided – I suppose it was my decision in a way, but greatly encouraged by them – that *Henry V* was a massively different problem from the other two, and had to be solved differently.'

The major difference between Part 1 and Part 2 as far as set designer Don Homfray was concerned was that the social scope of the play opens up. The most intense research needed, he recalls, was for the heraldry and details of warfare: 'That's what got previous productions into trouble.' But for him the interesting part of the research was 'getting under the skin of the middle ages'. Though the plays are historically set in the middle ages they are also social histories of Elizabethan England, and this was in the back of his mind while he was working on capturing the atmosphere of the middle ages – a double-think that he seems to have accepted quite happily. 'I tried to get the feel, the texture of the times – what sort of life it was: pretty awful, actually! You had to get that feeling before you could decide how much you were going to show. You just go on and on looking at pictures and eventually you begin to get a sense about how things would be. Design is an intuitive thing; you're trying to catch the flavour of the time. It's not really about historical fact, it's about the feeling you can get from the viewer by putting a certain thing on the screen. What is historically correct is not necessarily right for us because it may have all sorts of other connotations. All the time you're asking yourself what would be the connotations for a modern viewer if I put this on the screen?'

'The element, the detail, that makes *Henry IV Part 2* different from Part 1 is that you've got a middle-class thing and a country-life touch entering into the play with Justice Shallow and that lot, so that we've had to deviate slightly from the style of Part 1 to include some country interiors. But again we've tried to keep it simple, very simple; stripped to the basics. The two parts of *Henry IV* are two of my favourite plays, ever since I saw them at Stratford in the 1960s; but they're about images conjured up by poetry, not about scenery. The best thing the designer can do is create big arenas and let the actors get on with it, create a sort of atmosphere so the architecture and scenery aren't interfering in any way.'

For Part 1 costume designer Odette Barrow had had great difficulty with the research. Half-way through working on Part 2 she was able to make contact with a Yorkshireman, Charles Kightly, who had written a thesis on the clothes of Henry IV's reign and a book on the armour and clothes of the battle of Agincourt. So her research load was greatly lightened. She, too, allows herself a certain amount of licence, though not quite with such insouciance as Homfray. 'In those times there was a veto on what fabrics and furs you were allowed to wear, graded to your position in life. Below a certain level you were not allowed to wear your silks and satins and velvets. But you have to take a little bit of artistic licence here and there and break the rules sometimes, or it gets so bland. For instance, in Part 2 I had Doll Tearsheet in a very, very broken-down velvet dress – probably something that had been passed down and down; and since she was the whore of the tavern and probably thought herself a rather more high-class one, I thought it might be rather fun to put her in something that would have been picked up on the side somewhere, in very bad condition. Probably the purists will slam me for it,' she adds with a resigned sigh, used by now to being slammed by purists.

Another slight liberty she took was in the dressing of the Justices, Shallow and Silence. 'You have to look at the clothes of justices of that period but also work with the character. At that time a justice would have worn a coif, a little cap – but to put them both in caps would have made them look like Tweedledee and Tweedledum; so Shallow I put in a plain black hat without the coif. I tried to give the feel of what they were without putting them in full costume for court.'

'The most fun, of course, is working with the artist to get some feel of the character: it's a mistake to arrive with preconceived ideas about the work. Working with Anthony Quayle was enormous fun: the fittings were a couple of hours each time, first of all getting the basic padding, then seeing his movements so that you could work the padding on him. It was a complex creation, achieving those rolls of fat on the legs and arms but leaving his wrists and neck mobile and natural-looking. And Mr Quayle seemed to blend into the character, he became Falstaff!'

'And Bardolph – a lot of his stuff wasn't designed. I had lots and lots of pieces, and the actor [Gordon Gostelow] and I built up the costume together layer by layer, out of the weirdest garments. Working together that way you can come up with something that's very strange but very right: somehow the costume has built up a character.'

Henry IV Part 2 is, Alan Shallcross surprised me by pointing out, the fourth-longest play in the Shakespearian canon; but, also surprisingly, it presented fewer problems of cutting than the slightly short *Henry V*. 'In Part 2 one was able to cut in quite large chunks because the rhetoric of the argument in Gaultree forest scene is *en bloc*. Anyone who has produced the play will tell you that they go on and on and on about the politics and the morality: all talk and no action. The length of the interchange between the warring factions does make the centre of the play extremely static, so that has been a major candidate for excision. We cut almost nothing of the comic scenes, but what we tried to do was get the play into action quickly, so we excised a good deal of the opening scene. Those cuts consisted mostly of references to what has already happened, and because we were able to use a flashback technique we didn't need the words.'

Part 2, Giles points out, is crucial to an understanding of Henry the man in *Henry V*. 'If you see the repudiation of Falstaff in Part 2 it makes Henry absolutely different – one understands him and what he has done to himself in repudiating that side of his life. All through Part 2 Hal has much less to do with Falstaff and is obviously coming to the end of his companions because nobody measures up to Hotspur – whom he killed in Part 1 – at all. Then the king dies and the sad thing is they both go through that huge scene where Hal appears to steal the crown and Henry just lashes him with reproaches; then Hal explains himself and they come to a point, just before the king's death, where they actually start communicating. For about three minutes, because the king is dying and because they have worn each other down, they communicate – and then the king dies. It is wonderfully human and very tragic. Then Hal, as soon as he becomes king, has to cut Falstaff off. He cuts that side of himself off and becomes Henry V.'

Anthony Quayle, returning to the part of Falstaff which he first played more than quarter of a century ago at Stratford, sees this repudiation of Falstaff as crucial to Shakespeare's design in the three plays. The scene has long upset many who would like Henry V to be a more sentimental hero, but Quayle finds the moral choice wholly satisfying and wholly right. 'In Part 2 you find for the first time all kinds of things are happening to Falstaff. To begin with there is no hint of illness in Part 1. He may puff and pant a bit at Gadshill but he's robust: he marches, godamit, all the way to Shrewsbury and, though a coward, he gets into that melee on foot, all twenty-five stone of him, or whatever he weighs on the hoof. He never has even a cold – he has one scene where he says: "Do I not bate? Do I not dwindle? Why, my skin hangs about me like an old lady's loose gown; I am withered like an old apple-john", but that is really only very temporary. But in the very first scene of Part 2 he says: "What says the doctor to my water?" and the little page says: "He said, sir, the water itself was a good healthy water; but, for the party that owed it, he might have more diseases than he knew for." So from the very first scene he's discussing disease and there's a black edge all the time. At the end of that scene he says: "I will turn diseases to commodity," and all the way through there's sickness and he's preoccupied with death. Even in the scene with Doll Tearsheet he says: "Peace, good Doll! Do not speak like a death's-head; do not bid me remember mine end." He's *desperately* preoccupied with sickness and death. He's also –

there are signs of moral decay as well as physical decay: the speech about his ragamuffins in Part 1 – "Food for powder, food for powder," – is cynical but it's delivered with panache. But when you come to the recruiting scene in Part 2 the cynicism with which he deals with those miserable pressed recruits is tipping into blackness, as is the utter cynicism with which he fleeces Shallow. His relationship with Hal is frightfully good-natured in Part 1, but Shakespeare only gives them one scene together in Part 2 and Falstaff doesn't win the prince round at all! The prince is very cutting in the brief scene they have, and Hal's remarks about Falstaff are not at all affectionate.'

'That's all from a subjective point of view. Viewed externally, Shakespeare seems somewhere to have decided to go on to write the heroic, nationalistic play of *Henry V* and he's going to turn Hal, who's a rake in Part 1, into the national hero of *Henry V*. He *cannot* have Falstaff hanging round his neck – partly because the character of Falstaff is too rich and too ripe and would overshadow Henry. Shakespeare knows he's created too great a character, so he's got to get rid of him: partly because he can't have a hero who's going to win the Battle of Agincourt still trailing clouds of juvenile delinquency. So I think he quite deliberately in Part 2 gets rid of Falstaff. Part 1 seems to me to be a *feu de joie* and then he thinks "Hey, I'm getting myself into a lot of trouble; I've written a character who's in danger of running away with the whole caboodle. If I'm going to lead through Part 2 into *Henry V* I've got to get rid of this old b . . . Well, I'm going to start then to show that unbridled joyous licence is something actually corrupt. I'm going to write a play about honour and how do I reconcile that with Falstaff's speech about honour? How can you write *Henry V* and retain a character who can speak with such utter cynicism? Though attractive, fascinating as that point of view may be – amusing, funny, something that we all know – by the time I come to *Henry V* I've got to show a dark side and Hal has got to disown him." And that is what Shakespeare therefore has him do.

'I think the audience must love Falstaff to the end but they must also say: "Hal had to do that, he really had to!" When a man can say: "The laws of England are at my commandment. Blessed are they that have been my friends; and woe to my Lord Chief Justice!" Well! In the first part he's the most heavenly balloon but the balloon in Part 2 has overreached himself and he's saying, "I've got the king in my pocket". There's a smell about Falstaff of decay.' David Gwillim, playing the controversial Hal, brings a clear-eyed logic to the part and conveys an impression of intense seriousness and scrupulous honesty in his approach to the character and to the play's moral dilemmas. By odd coincidence he and Anthony Quayle have known each other since Gwillim's childhood, when his father, Jack Gwillim, was in the company at Stratford that performed the *Henry IV* in which Quayle first played Falstaff. Though this intimacy may warm Quayle's performance one doesn't feel that it would be likely to touch Gwillim's. In spite of the intricacy of the character of Hal, the role in Part 2, he points out with almost apologetic exactness, 'tis not a huge role to play. It's a very nice role but it's not huge. In Part 2 the progression of the times you see Hal throughout the play covers, in reality, a period of eight years. Now that period is covered by one costume that I wear – quite rightly, because the attitude is identical and he changes the costume when he changes the attitude!'

'Part 2 is a process of getting rid of people. He gets rid of Poins, he gets rid of Falstaff. I suppose he is shedding the crysalis. It can be seen as an act of self-involved weakness but I don't think it should be. Falstaff would be a disaster for England and I think it will be very clear from Tony's performance just how terrible it would be. With Hal's father's neurosis about what's going to happen, I think there should be a certain satisfaction when the errant boy comes home. But while the logical conclusion to that coming home may be good, I do think his dealing with Poins is very cruel. His dealing with Falstaff, on the other hand, destroys Falstaff but there's no intention to be cruel; there's just a statement of truth: "I can't associate with you." It's as simple as that. Which makes it awful! It's awful and painful for everybody. But it's a logical conclusion; it's what has to happen. Maybe it is in some respects unsympathetic, but I'm not sure what would be sympathetic! Certainly I don't see Hal as a shining knight; I do see him as ruthless.' But, he seems to imply, is that so bad when it leads to the creation of the character of Henry V? And is not that at least a major part of Shakespeare's point?

THE BBC TV CAST AND PRODUCTION TEAM

The cast for the BBC television production was as follows:

KING HENRY IV	Jon Finch
HENRY, PRINCE OF WALES	David Gwillim
JOHN OF LANCASTER	Rob Edwards
HUMPHREY OF GLOUCESTER	Martin Neil
THOMAS, DUKE OF CLARENCE	Roger Davenport
EARL OF NORTHUMBERLAND	Bruce Purchase
SCROOP, ARCHBISHOP OF YORK	David Neal
LORD MOWBRAY	Michael Miller
LORD HASTINGS	Richard Bebb
LORD BARDOLPH	John Humphry
SIR JOHN COLVILLE	Salvin Stewart
TRAVERS	David Strong
MORTON	Carl Oatley
EARL OF WARWICK	Rod Beacham
EARL OF WESTMORELAND	David Buck
GOWER	Brian Poyser
LORD CHIEF JUSTICE	Ralph Michael
SIR JOHN FALSTAFF	Anthony Quayle
POINS	Jack Galloway
BARDOLPH	Gordon Gostelow
PISTOL	Bryan Pringle
PETO	Steven Beard
PAGE	John Fowler
ROBERT SHALLOW	Robert Eddison
SILENCE	Leslie French
DAVY	Raymond Platt
FANG	Frederick Proud
RALPH MOULDY	Julian Battersby
SIMON SHADOW	Roy Herrick
THOMAS WART	Alan Collins

FRANCIS FEEBLE	John Tordoff
PETER BULLCALF	Roger Elliott
LADY NORTHUMBERLAND	Jenny Laird
LADY PERCY	Michele Dotrice
MISTRESS QUICKLY	Brenda Bruce
DOLL TEARSHEET	Frances Cuka
SERVANT	Tim Brown
MESSENGER	Colin Dunn
PRODUCTION ASSISTANT	Jenny Macarthur
DIRECTOR'S ASSISTANT	Beryl Watts
PRODUCTION UNIT MANAGER	Fraser Lowden
MUSIC ADVISER	David Lloyd-Jones
LITERARY CONSULTANT	John Wilders
MAKE-UP ARTIST	Elizabeth Moss
COSTUME DESIGNER	Odette Barrow
SOUND	Colin Dixon
LIGHTING	Dennis Channon
DESIGNER	Don Homfray
SCRIPT EDITOR	Alan Shallcross
PRODUCER	Cedric Messina
DIRECTOR	David Giles

The production was recorded between 11 and 16 April 1979.

THE TEXT

In order to help readers who might wish to use this text to follow the play on the screen the scene divisions and locations used in the television production and any cuts and rearrangements made are shown in the right-hand margins. The principles governing these annotations are as follows:

1. Where a new location (change of set) is used by the TV production this is shown as a new scene. The scenes are numbered consecutively, and each one is identified as exterior or interior, located by a brief description of the set of the location, and placed in its 'time' setting (e.g. Day, Night, Dawn). These procedures are those used in BBC Television camera scripts.

2. Where the original stage direction shows the entry of a character at the beginning of a scene, this has not been deleted (unless it causes confusion). This is in order to demonstrate which characters are in the scene, since in most cases the TV scene begins with the characters 'discovered' on the set.

3. Where the start of a TV scene does not coincide with the start of a scene in the printed text, the characters in that scene have been listed, *unless* the start of the scene coincides with a stage direction which indicates the entrance of all those characters.

4. Where the text has been cut in the TV production, the cuts are marked by vertical rules and by a note in the margin. If complete lines are cut these are shown as, e.g., Lines 27–38 omitted. If part of a line only is cut, or in cases of doubt (e.g. in prose passages), the first and last words of the cut are also given.

5. Occasionally, and only when it is thought necessary for comprehension of the action, a note of a character's moves has been inserted in the margin.

6. Where the action moves from one part of a set to another, no attempt has been made to show this as a succession of scenes.

ALAN SHALLCROSS

2 HENRY IV

DRAMATIS PERSONÆ

RUMOUR, *the Presenter.*
KING HENRY THE FOURTH
HENRY, PRINCE OF
WALES, *afterwards*
HENRY V,
PRINCE JOHN OF LANCAS-
TER,
PRINCE HUMPHREY OF
GLOUCESTER,
THOMAS, DUKE OF CLAR-
ENCE,

sons of Henry IV.

EARL OF NORTHUMBER-
LAND,
SCROOP, ARCHBISHOP OF
YORK,
LORD MOWBRAY,
LORD HASTINGS,
LORD BARDOLPH,
SIR JOHN COLVILLE,

opposites against King Henry IV.

TRAVERS,
MORTON,

retainers of Northumber-land,

EARL OF WARWICK,
EARL OF WESTMORELAND,
EARL OF SURREY,
* EARL OF KENT,
GOWER,
* HARCOURT,
* BLUNT,
LORD CHIEF JUSTICE.
Servant, *to Lord Chief Justice.*

of the King's party.

SIR JOHN FALSTAFF,
EDWARD POINS,
BARDOLPH,
PISTOL,
PETO,
Page, *to Falstaff.*

irregular Humourists.

ROBERT SHALLOW,
SILENCE,

country Justices.

DAVY, *servant to Shallow.*
FANG,
† SNARE,

Sheriff's officers.

RALPH MOULDY,
SIMON SHADOW,
THOMAS WART,
FRANCIS FEEBLE,
PETER BULLCALF,
* FRANCIS, *a drawer.*

country soldiers.

LADY NORTHUMBERLAND.
LADY PERCY, *Percy's widow.*
HOSTESS QUICKLY, *of the Boar's Head, Eastcheap.*
DOLL TEARSHEET.

Lords, Attendants, Porter, Drawers, Beadles, Grooms, Servants.

* In the television production these parts are omitted.

† Non-speaking part in the television production.

Before the play opens we see, in flashback, King Richard II handing the Crown of England to Bolingbroke.

[Mix to]

Bolingbroke (now King Henry IV) at his prayers.

[Mix to]

Prince Hal in mortal combat with Hotspur on Shrewsbury field. Over these pictures we hear the voice of RUMOUR.

THE SCENE : *England.*

INDUCTION.

Warkworth. Before Northumberland's castle.

Enter RUMOUR, *painted full of tongues.*

RUM. Open your ears ; for which of you will stop
The vent of hearing when loud Rumour speaks ?
I, from the orient to the drooping west,
Making the wind my post-horse, still unfold
The acts commenced on this ball of earth.   5
Upon my tongues continual slanders ride,
The which in every language I pronounce,
Stuffing the ears of men with false reports.

Lines 6–22 omitted.

I speak of peace while covert enmity,
Under the smile of safety, wounds the world; 10
And who but Rumour, who but only I,
Make fearful musters and prepar'd defence,
Whiles the big year, swoln with some other grief,
Is thought with child by the stern tyrant war,
And no such matter? Rumour is a pipe 15
Blown by surmises, jealousies, conjectures,
And of so easy and so plain a stop
That the blunt monster with uncounted heads,
The still-discordant wav'ring multitude
Can play upon it. But what need I thus 20
My well-known body to anatomize
Among my household? Why is Rumour here?
I run before King Harry's victory,
Who, in a bloody field by Shrewsbury,
Hath beaten down young Hotspur and his troops, 25
Quenching the flame of bold rebellion
Even with the rebels' blood. But what mean I
To speak so true at first? My office is
To noise abroad that Harry Monmouth fell
Under the wrath of noble Hotspur's sword, 30
And that the King before the Douglas' rage
Stoop'd his anointed head as low as death.
This have I rumour'd through the peasant towns
Between that royal field of Shrewsbury
* And this worm-eaten hold of ragged stone, 35
Where Hotspur's father, old Northumberland,
Lies crafty-sick. The posts come tiring on,
And not a man of them brings other news
Than they have learnt of me. From Rumour's tongues
They bring smooth comforts false, worse than true wrongs. [*Exit.*

ACT ONE.

SCENE I. *Warkworth. Before Northumberland's castle.*

Enter LORD BARDOLPH.

L. BARD. Who keeps the gate here, ho?

The Porter *opens the gate.*

Where is the Earl?
PORT. What shall I say you are?
L. BARD. Tell thou the Earl
That the Lord Bardolph doth attend him here.
PORT. His lordship is walk'd forth into the orchard.
Please it your honour knock but at the gate,
And he himself will answer

Enter NORTHUMBERLAND.

L. BARD. Here comes the Earl. [*Exit* Porter.
NORTH. What news, Lord Bardolph? Every minute now
Should be the father of some strategem.
The times are wild; contention, like a horse

Lines 6–22 omitted.

* Line 35:
The voice of RUMOUR
continues over:
SCENE I
*Interior. A Room in
Warkworth Castle.
Day.*
NORTHUMBERLAND,
LADY
NORTHUMBERLAND.
They hear LORD
BARDOLPH's approach
and LADY
NORTHUMBERLAND
goes out to greet him.

At line 39:
SCENE 2
*Interior. A Staircase in
Warkworth Castle.
Day.*
LORD BARDOLPH
greets LADY
NORTHUMBERLAND.

SCENE 3
*Interior. A Room in
Warkworth Castle.
Day.*
NORTHUMBERLAND,
LORD BARDOLPH.

Lines 1–6 omitted.

Full of high feeding, madly hath broke loose   10
And bears down all before him.
L. BARD.   Noble Earl,
I bring you certain news from Shrewsbury.
NORTH. Good, an God will!
L. BARD. As good as heart can wish.
The King is almost wounded to the death;   15
And, in the fortune of my lord your son,
Prince Harry slain outright; and both the Blunts
Kill'd by the hand of Douglas; young Prince John,
And Westmoreland, and Stafford, fled the field;
And Harry Monmouth's brawn, the hulk Sir John
Is prisoner to your son. O, such a day,   20
So fought, so followed, and so fairly won,
Came not till now to dignify the times,
Since Cæsar's fortunes!
NORTH.   How is this deriv'd?
Saw you the field? Came you from Shrewsbury?
L. BARD. I spake with one, my lord, that came from thence;   25
A gentleman well bred and of good name,
That freely rend'red me these news for true.

Enter TRAVERS.

NORTH. Here comes my servant Travers, whom I sent
On Tuesday last to listen after news.
L. BARD. My lord, I over-rode him on the way;   30
And he is furnish'd with no certainties
More than he haply may retail from me.
NORTH. Now, Travers, what good tidings come with you?
TRA. My lord, Sir John Umfrevile turn'd me back
With joyful tidings; and, being better hors'd,   35
Out-rode me. After him came spurring hard
A gentleman, almost forspent with speed,
That stopp'd by me to breathe his bloodied horse.
He ask'd the way to Chester; and of him
I did demand what news from Shrewsbury.   40
He told me that rebellion had bad luck,
And that young Harry Percy's spur was cold.
With that he gave his able horse the head
And, bending forward, struck his armed heels
Against the panting sides of his poor jade   45
Up to the rowel-head; and starting so,
He seem'd in running to devour the way,
Staying no longer question.
NORTH.   Ha! Again:
Said he young Harry Percy's spur was cold?
Of Hotspur, Coldspur? that rebellion   50
Had met ill luck?
L. BARD.   My lord, I'll tell you what:
If my young lord your son have not the day,
Upon mine honour, for a silken point
I'll give my barony. Never talk of it.
NORTH. Why should that gentleman that rode by Travers   55
Give then such instances of loss?

Lines 16–23,
'outright; and both
. . . Cæsar's
fortunes', omitted.

Lines 28–33 omitted.

Lines 34, 'Sir John
. . .', to 36 omitted.

'That' omitted.

Lines 43–51, '. . . ill
luck', omitted.

Lines 55–59 omitted.

L. BARD.   Who—he ?
  He was some hilding fellow that had stol'n
  The horse he rode on and, upon my life,
  Spoke at a venture.   Look, here comes more news.

Enter MORTON.

NORTH. Yea, this man's brow, like to a title-leaf,   60
  Foretells the nature of a tragic volume.
  So looks the strand whereon the imperious flood
  Hath left a witness'd usurpation.
  Say, Morton, didst thou come from Shrewsbury ?
MOR. I ran from Shrewsbury, my noble lord ;   65
  Where hateful death put on his ugliest mask
  To fright our party.
NORTH. How doth my son and brother ?
  Thou tremblest ; and the whiteness in thy cheek
  Is apter than thy tongue to tell thy errand.
  Even such a man, so faint, so spiritless,   70
  So dull, so dead in look, so woe-begone,
  Drew Priam's curtain in the dead of night
  And would have told him half his Troy was burnt ;
  But Priam found the fire ere he his tongue,
  And I my Percy's death ere thou report'st it.   75
  This thou wouldst say : ' Your son did thus and thus ;
  Your brother thus ; so fought the noble Douglas '—
  Stopping my greedy ear with their bold deeds ;
  But in the end, to stop my ear indeed,
  Thou hast a sigh to blow away this praise,   80
  Ending with ' Brother, son, and all, are dead '.
MOR. Douglas is living, and your brother, yet ;
  But for my lord your son—
NORTH.   Why, he is dead.
  See what a ready tongue suspicion hath !
  He that but fears the thing he would not know   85
  Hath by instinct knowledge from others' eyes
  That what he fear'd is chanced.   Yet speak, Morton ;
  Tell thou an earl his divination lies,
  And I will take it as a sweet disgrace
  And make thee rich for doing me such wrong.   90
MOR. You are too great to be by me gainsaid ;
  Your spirit is too true, your fears too certain.
NORTH. Yet, for all this, say not that Percy's dead.
  I see a strange confession in thine eye ;
  Thou shak'st thy head, and hold'st it fear or sin   95
  To speak a truth.   If he be slain, say so
  The tongue offends not that reports his death ;
  And he doth sin that doth belie the dead,
  Not he which says the dead is not alive.
  Yet the first bringer of unwelcome news   100
  Hath but a losing office, and his tongue
  Sounds ever after as a sullen bell,
  Rememb'red tolling a departing friend.
L. BARD. I cannot think, my lord, your son is dead.
MOR. I am sorry I should force you to believe   105

Lines 55–59 omitted.

TRAVERS. My Lord, I
spoke with one
who . . .

Lines 62–63 omitted.

Lines 70–81 omitted.

Lines 85–103
omitted.

Bruce Purchase (left) as the Earl of Northumberland and John Humphry (right) as Lord Bardolph

Frances Cuka as Doll Tearsheet and Brenda Bruce as Mistress Quickly

That which I would to God I had not seen ;
But these mine eyes saw him in bloody state,
Rend'ring faint quittance, wearied and out-breath'd,
To Harry Monmouth, whose swift wrath beat down
The never-daunted Percy to the earth,   110
From whence with life he never more sprung up.
In few, his death—whose spirit lent a fire
Even to the dullest peasant in his camp—
Being bruited once, took fire and heat away
From the best-temper'd courage in his troops ;   115
For from his metal was his party steeled ;
Which once in him abated, all the rest
Turn'd on themselves, like dull and heavy lead.
And as the thing that's heavy in itself
Upon enforcement flies with greatest speed,   120
So did our men, heavy in Hotspur's loss,
Lend to this weight such lightness with their fear
That arrows fled not swifter toward their aim
Than did our soldiers, aiming at their safety,
Fly from the field.   Then was that noble Worcester   125
Too soon ta'en prisoner ; and that furious Scot,
The bloody Douglas, whose well labouring sword
Had three times slain th' appearance of the King,
Gan vail his stomach and did grace the shame
Of those that turn'd their backs, and in his flight,   130
Stumbling in fear, was took.   The sum of all
Is that the King hath won, and hath sent out
A speedy power to encounter you, my lord,
Under the conduct of young Lancaster
And Westmoreland.   This is the news at full.   135
NORTH. For this I shall have time enough to mourn.
In poison there is physic ; and these news,
Having been well, that would have made me sick,
Being sick, have in some measure made me well ;
And as the wretch whose fever-weak'ned joints,   140
Like strengthless hinges, buckle under life,
Impatient of his fit, breaks like a fire
Out of his keeper's arms, even so my limbs,
Weak'ned with grief, being now enrag'd with grief,
Are thrice themselves.   Hence, therefore, thou nice crutch ! 145
A scaly gauntlet now with joints of steel
Must glove this hand ; and hence, thou sickly coif !
Thou art a guard too wanton for the head
Which princes, flesh'd with conquest, aim to hit.
Now bind my brows with iron ; and approach   150
The ragged'st hour that time and spite dare bring
To frown upon th' enrag'd Northumberland !
Let heaven kiss earth !   Now let not Nature's hand
Keep the wild flood confin'd !   Let order die !
And let this world no longer be a stage   155
To feed contention in a ling'ring act ;
But let one spirit of the first-born Cain
Reign in all bosoms, that, each heart being set
On bloody courses, the rude scene may end

Lines 112–135
omitted.

Lines 140–149
omitted.

And darkness be the burier of the dead !   160
L. BARD. This strained passion doth you wrong, my lord.
MOR. Sweet Earl, divorce not wisdom from your honour.   Lines 162–179
    The lives of all your loving complices   omitted.
    Lean on your health ; the which, if you give o'er
    To stormy passion, must perforce decay.   165
    You cast th' event of war, my noble lord,
    And summ'd the account of chance before you said
    'Let us make head'.   It was your pre-surmise
    That in the dole of blows your son might drop.
    You knew he walk'd o'er perils on an edge,   170
    More likely to fall in than to get o'er ;
    You were advis'd his flesh was capable
    Of wounds and scars, and that his forward spirit
    Would lift him where most trade of danger rang'd ;
    Yet did you say ' Go forth ' ; and none of this,   175
    Though strongly apprehended, could restrain
    The stiff-borne action.   What hath then befall'n,
    Or what hath this bold enterprise brought forth
    More than that being which was like to be ?
L. BARD. We all that are engaged to this loss   180
    Knew that we ventured on such dangerous seas
    That if we wrought out life 'twas ten to one ;
    And yet we ventur'd, for the gain propos'd
    Chok'd the respect of likely peril fear'd ;
    And since we are o'erset, venture again.   185
    Come, we will put forth, body and goods.
MOR. 'Tis more than time.   And, my most noble lord,
    I hear for certain, and dare speak the truth :
    The gentle Archbishop of York is up
    With well-appointed pow'rs.   He is a man   190   Lines 190–200, 'He is
    Who with a double surety binds his followers.   a man . . . now the
    My lord your son had only but the corpse,   Bishop', omitted.
    But shadows and the shows of men, to fight ;
    For that same word ' rebellion ' did divide
    The action of their bodies from their souls ;   195
    And they did fight with queasiness, constrain'd,
    As men drink potions ; that their weapons only
    Seem'd on our side, but for their spirits and souls
    This word ' rebellion '—it had froze them up,
    As fish are in a pond.   But now the Bishop   200
    Turns insurrection to religion.
    Suppos'd sincere and holy in his thoughts,
    He's follow'd both with body and with mind ;
    And doth enlarge his rising with the blood
    Of fair King Richard, scrap'd from Pomfret stones ;   205
    Derives from heaven his quarrel and his cause ;
    Tells them he doth bestride a bleeding land,
    Gasping for life under great Bolingbroke ;
    And more and less do flock to follow him.
NORTH. I knew of this before ; but, to speak truth,   210
    This present grief had wip'd it from my mind.
    Go in with me ; and counsel every man
    The aptest way for safety and revenge.

Get posts and letters, and make friends with speed—
Never so few, and never yet more need.   [*Exeunt.*]

Lines 214–215
omitted.

SCENE II. *London. A street.*

Enter SIR JOHN FALSTAFF, *with his* Page *bearing his sword and buckler.*

SCENE 4
*Exterior. London.
A Street. Day.*

FAL. Sirrah, you giant, what says the doctor to my water ?

PAGE. He said, sir, the water itself was a good healthy water ; but for the party that owed it, he might have moe diseases than he knew for.

FAL. Men of all sorts take a pride to gird at me. The brain of this foolish-compounded clay, man, is not able to invent anything that intends to laughter, more than I invent or is invented on me. I am not only witty in myself, but the cause that wit is in other men. I do here walk before thee like a sow that hath overwhelm'd all her litter but one. If the Prince put thee into my service for any other reason than to set me off, why then I have no judgment. Thou whoreson mandrake, thou art fitter to be worn in my cap than to wait at my heels. I was never mann'd with an agate till now ; but I will inset you neither in gold nor silver, but in vile apparel, and send you back again to your master, for a jewel—the juvenal, the Prince your master, whose chin is not yet fledge. I will sooner have a beard grow in the palm of my hand than he shall get one off his cheek ; and yet he will not stick to say his face is a face-royal. God may finish it when he will, 'tis not a hair amiss yet. He may keep it still at a face-royal, for a barber shall never earn sixpence out of it ; and yet he'll be crowing as if he had writ man ever since his father was a bachelor. He may keep his own grace, but he's almost out of mine, I can assure him. What said Master Dommelton about the satin for my short cloak and my slops ?   28

'I was never mann'd
. . . assure him'
omitted.

PAGE. He said, sir, you should procure him better assurance than Bardolph. He would not take his band and yours ; he liked not the security.

FAL. Let him be damn'd, like the Glutton ; pray God his tongue be hotter ! A whoreson Achitophel ! A rascal-yea-forsooth knave, to bear a gentleman in hand, and then stand upon security ! The whoreson smooth-pates do now wear nothing but high shoes, and bunches of keys at their girdles ; and if a man is through with them in honest taking-up, then they must stand upon security. I had as lief they would put ratsbane in my mouth as offer to stop it with security. I look'd 'a should have sent me two and twenty yards of satin, as I am a true knight, and he sends me security. Well, he may sleep in security ; for he hath the horn of abundance, and the lightness of his wife shines through it ; and yet cannot he see, though he have his own lanthorn to light him. Where's Bardolph ?   45

'Let him . . . be
hotter!' omitted.
'The whoreson . . .
upon security'
omitted.

'I look'd 'a . . . to
light him' omitted.

PAGE He's gone into Smithfield to buy your worship a horse.

FAL. I bought him in Paul's, and he'll buy me a horse in Smithfield. An I could get me but a wife in the stews, I were mann'd, hors'd, and wiv'd.

Enter the LORD CHIEF JUSTICE *and* Servant.

PAGE. Sir, here comes the nobleman that committed the Prince for
striking him about Bardolph.
FAL. Wait close ; I will not see him.
CH. JUSTICE. What's he that goes there ?
SERV. Falstaff, an't please your lordship.   55
CH. JUST. He that was in question for the robb'ry ?
SERV. He, my lord ; but he hath since done good service at Shrews-
bury, and, as I hear, is now going with some charge to the Lord
John of Lancaster.
CH. JUST. What, to York ?   Call him back again.   60
SERV. Sir John Falstaff !
FAL. Boy, tell him I am deaf.
PAGE. You must speak louder ; my master is deaf.
CH. JUST. I am sure he is, to the hearing of anything good.   Go,
pluck him by the elbow ; I must speak with him.   66
SERV. Sir John !
FAL. What ! a young knave, and begging !   Is there not wars ?   Is
there not employment ?   Doth not the King lack subjects ?   Do
not the rebels need soldiers ?   Though it be a shame to be on any
side but one, it is worse shame to beg than to be on the worst side,
were it worse than the name of rebellion can tell how to make it.
SERV. You mistake me, sir.   74
FAL. Why, sir, did I say you were an honest man ?   Setting my
knighthood and my soldiership aside, I had lied in my throat
if I had said so.
SERV. I pray you, sir, then set your knighthood and your soldiership
aside ; and give me leave to tell you you lie in your throat, if you
say I am any other than an honest man.   81
FAL. I give thee leave to tell me so ! I lay aside that which grows
to me ! If thou get'st any leave of me, hang me ; if thou tak'st
leave, thou wert better be hang'd.   You hunt counter.   Hence !
Avaunt !   85
SERV. Sir, my lord would speak with you.
CH. JUST. Sir John Falstaff, a word with you.
FAL. My good lord !   God give your lordship good time of day.   I
am glad to see your lordship abroad.   I heard say your lordship
was sick ; I hope your lordship goes abroad by advice.   Your
lordship, though not clean past your youth, hath yet some smack
of age in you, some relish of the saltness of time ; and I most
humbly beseech your lordship to have a reverend care of your
health.
CH. JUST. Sir John, I sent for you before your expedition to Shrewsbury.   96
FAL. An't please your lordship, I hear his Majesty is return'd with
some discomfort from Wales.
CH. JUST. I talk not of his Majesty.   You would not come when I
sent for you.   100
FAL. And I hear, moreover, his Highness is fall'n into this same whore-
son apoplexy.
CH. JUST. Well, God mend him !   I pray you let me speak with you.
FAL. This apoplexy, as I take it, is a kind of lethargy, an't please your
lordship, a kind of sleeping in the blood, a whoreson tingling.
CH. JUST. What tell you me of it ?   Be it as it is.
FAL. It hath it original from much grief, from study, and perturbation

Lines 69–85, 'Doth
not the King . . .
Avaunt!', omitted.

of the brain. I have read the cause of his effects in Galen ; it is a
kind of deafness.   111

CH. JUST. I think you are fall'n into the disease, for you hear not what
I say to you.

FAL. Very well, my lord, very well. Rather an't please you, it is the
disease of not listening, the malady of not marking, that I am
troubled withal.   116

CH. JUST. To punish you by the heels would amend the attention of
your ears ; and I care not if I do become your physician.

FAL. I am as poor as Job, my lord, but not so patient. Your lordship
may minister the potion of imprisonment to me in respect of
poverty ; but how I should be your patient to follow your
prescriptions, the wise may make some dram of a scruple, or
indeed a scruple itself.   124

CH. JUST. I sent for you, when there were matters against you for
your life, to come speak with me.

FAL. As I was then advis'd by my learned counsel in the laws of this
land-service, I did not come.

CH. JUST. Well, the truth is, Sir John, you live in great infamy.

FAL. He that buckles himself in my belt cannot live in less.

CH. JUST. Your means are very slender, and your waste is great.

FAL. I would it were otherwise ; I would my means were greater and
my waist slenderer.   135

CH. JUST. You have misled the youthful Prince.

FAL. The young Prince hath misled me. I am the fellow with the
great belly, and he my dog.

CH. JUST. Well, I am loath to gall a new-heal'd wound. Your day's
service at Shrewsbury hath a little gilded over your night's exploit
on Gadshill. You may thank th' unquiet time for your quiet
o'erposting that action.   142

FAL. My lord—

CH. JUST. But since all is well, keep it so : wake not a sleeping wolf.

FAL. To wake a wolf is as bad as smell a fox.

CH. JUST. What ! you are as a candle, the better part burnt out.

FAL. A wassail candle, my lord—all tallow ; if I did say of wax, my
growth would approve the truth.   150

CH. JUST. There is not a white hair in your face but should have his
effect of gravity.

FAL. His effect of gravy, gravy, gravy.

CH. JUST. You follow the young Prince up and down, like his ill angel.

FAL. Not so, my lord. Your ill angel is light ; but I hope he that
looks upon me will take me without weighing. And yet in some
respects, I grant, I cannot go—I cannot tell. Virtue is of so
little regard in these costermongers' times that true valour is
turn'd berod ; pregnancy is made a tapster, and his quick wit
wasted in giving reckonings ; all the other gifts appertinent to
man, as the malice of this age shapes them, are not worth a
gooseberry. You that are old consider not the capacities of us
that are young ; you do measure the heat of our livers with the
bitterness of your galls ; and we that are in the vaward of our
youth, I must confess, are wags too.   167

CH. JUST. Do you set down your name in the scroll of youth, that are
written down old with all the characters of age ? Have you not
a moist eye, a dry hand, a yellow cheek, a white beard, a decreasing

Lines 119–124, 'I am
as poor . . . scruple
itself', omitted.

'to come speak with
me' omitted.
'in the laws of this
land-service'
omitted.

'You may thank . . .
My lord – ' omitted.

'wake not a sleeping
wolf . . . gravy,
gravy' omitted.

'Your ill angel . . .
gooseberry' omitted.

'you do measure . . .
are wags too'
omitted.

leg, an increasing belly? Is not your voice broken, your wind
short, your chin double, your wit single, and every part about you
blasted with antiquity? And will you yet call yourself young?
Fie, fie, fie, Sir John!   175
FAL. My lord, I was born about three of the clock in the afternoon,
with a white head and something a round belly. For my voice—
I have lost it with hallooing and singing of anthems. To approve
my youth further, I will not. The truth is, I am only old in
judgment and understanding; and he that will caper with me
for a thousand marks, let him lend me the money, and have at him.
For the box of the ear that the Prince gave you—he gave it like a
rude prince, and you took it like a sensible lord. I have check'd
him for it; and the young lion repents—marry, not in ashes and
sackcloth, but in new silk and old sack.   186
CH. JUST. Well, God send the Prince a better companion!
FAL. God send the companion a better prince! I cannot rid my
hands of him.
CH. JUST. Well, the King hath sever'd you. I hear you are going
with Lord John of Lancaster against the Archbishop and the Earl
of Northumberland.   193
FAL. Yea; I thank your pretty sweet wit for it. But look you pray,
all you that kiss my Lady Peace at home, that our armies join not
in a hot day; for, by the Lord, I take but two shirts out with me,
and I mean not to sweat extraordinarily. If it be a hot day, and I   'If it be . . . white
brandish anything but a bottle, I would I might never spit white   again' omitted.
again. There is not a dangerous action can peep out his head but
I am thrust upon it. Well, I cannot last ever; but it was always
yet the trick of our English nation, if they have a good thing, to
make it too common. If ye will needs say I am an old man, you
should give me rest. I would to God my name were not so
terrible to the enemy as it is. I were better to be eaten to death
with a rust than to be scoured to nothing with perpetual motion.
CH. JUST. Well, be honest, be honest; and God bless your expedition!
FAL. Will your lordship lend me a thousand pound to furnish me
forth?   211
CH. JUST. Not a penny, not a penny; you are too impatient to bear   'you are too impatient
crosses. Fare you well. Commend me to my cousin Westmore-   to bear crosses'
land.   [Exeunt Chief Justice and Servant.   omitted.
FAL. If I do, fillip me with a three-man beetle. A man can no   'A man can . . . my
more separate age and covetousness than 'a can part young limbs   curses' omitted.
and lechery; but the gout galls the one, and the pox pinches the
other; and so both the degrees prevent my curses. Boy!
PAGE. Sir?   220
FAL. What money is in my purse?
PAGE. Seven groats and two pence.
FAL. I can get no remedy against this consumption of the purse;
borrowing only lingers and lingers it out, but the disease is
incurable. Go bear this letter to my Lord of Lancaster; this to
the Prince; this to the Earl of Westmoreland; and this to old
Mistress Ursula, whom I have weekly sworn to marry since I
perceiv'd the first white hair of my chin. About it; you know
where to find me. [Exit Page.] A pox of this gout! or, a gout of
this pox! for the one or the other plays the rogue with my great
toe. 'Tis no matter if I do halt; I have the wars for my colour,

and my pension shall seem the more reasonable.   A good wit will
make use of anything.   I will turn diseases to commodity. [*Exit.*

SCENE III.   *York.   The Archbishop's palace.*

Enter the ARCHBISHOP, THOMAS MOWBRAY *the* EARL MARSHAL, LORD
HASTINGS *and* LORD BARDOLPH.

ARCH. Thus have you heard our cause and known our means;
  And, my most noble friends, I pray you all
  Speak plainly your opinions of our hopes—
  And first, Lord Marshal, what say you to it?
MOWB. I well allow the occasion of our arms;   5
  But gladly would be better satisfied
  How, in our means, we should advance ourselves
  To look with forehead bold and big enough
  Upon the power and puissance of the King.
HAST. Our present musters grow upon the file   10
  To five and twenty thousand men of choice;
  And our supplies live largely in the hope
  Of great Northumberland, whose bosom burns
  With an incensed fire of injuries.
L. BARD. The question then, Lord Hastings, standeth thus: 15
  Whether our present five and twenty thousand
  May hold up head without Northumberland?
HAST. With him, we may.
L. BARD. Yea, marry, there's the point;
  But if without him we be thought too feeble,
  My judgment is we should not step too far   20
  Till we had his assistance by the hand;
  For, in a theme so bloody-fac'd as this,
  Conjecture, expectation, and surmise
  Of aids incertain, should not be admitted.
ARCH. 'Tis very true, Lord Bardolph; for indeed   25
  It was young Hotspur's case at Shrewsbury.
L. BARD. It was, my lord; who lin'd himself with hope,
  Eating the air and promise of supply,
  Flatt'ring himself in project of a power
  Much smaller than the smallest of his thoughts;   30
  And so, with great imagination
  Proper to madmen, led his powers to death,
  And, winking, leapt into destruction.
HAST. But, by your leave, it never yet did hurt
  To lay down likelihoods and forms of hope.   35
L. BARD. Yes, if this present quality of war—
  Indeed the instant action, a cause on foot—
  Lives so in hope, as in an early spring
  We see th' appearing buds; which to prove fruit
  Hope gives not so much warrant, as despair   40
  That frosts will bite them.   When we mean to build,
  We first survey the plot, then draw the model;
  And when we see the figure of the house,
  Then we must rate the cost of the erection;
  Which if we find outweighs ability,   45
  What do we then but draw anew the model

SCENE 5
*Interior. York. The
Archbishop's Palace.
Day.*

Lines 4–9 omitted.

Lines 36–65 omitted.

In fewer offices, or at least desist
To build at all ?   Much more, in this great work—
Which is almost to pluck a kingdom down
And set another up—should we survey   50
The plot of situation and the model,
Consent upon a sure foundation,
Question surveyors, know our own estate
How able such a work to undergo—
To weigh against his opposite ; or else   55
We fortify in paper and in figures,
Using the names of men instead of men ;
Like one that draws the model of a house
Beyond his power to build it ; who, half through,
Gives o'er and leaves his part-created cost   60
A naked subject to the weeping clouds
And waste for churlish winter's tyranny.
HAST. Grant that our hopes—yet likely of fair birth—
Should be still-born, and that we now possess'd
The utmost man of expectation,   65
I think we are so a body strong enough,
Even as we are, to equal with the King.
L. BARD. What, is the King but five and twenty thousand ?
HAST. To us no more ; nay, not so much, Lord Bardolph ;
For his divisions, as the times do brawl,   70
Are in three heads : one power against the French,
And one against Glendower ; perforce a third
Must take up us.   So is the unfirm King
In three divided ; and his coffers sound
With hollow poverty and emptiness.   75
ARCH. That he should draw his several strengths together
And come against us in full puissance
Need not be dreaded.
HAST.   If he should do so,
He leaves his back unarm'd, the French and Welsh
Baying at his heels.   Never fear that.   80
L. BARD. Who is it like should lead his forces hither ?
HAST. The Duke of Lancaster and Westmoreland ;
Against the Welsh, himself and Harry Monmouth ;
But who is substituted against the French
I have no certain notice.
ARCH.   Let us on,   85
And publish the occasion of our arms.
The commonwealth is sick of their own choice ;
Their over-greedy love hath surfeited.
An habitation giddy and unsure
Hath he that buildeth on the vulgar heart.   90
O thou fond many, with what loud applause
Didst thou beat heaven with blessing Bolingbroke
Before he was what thou wouldst have him be !
And being now trimm'd in thine own desires,
Thou, beastly feeder, art so full of him   95
That thou provok'st thyself to cast him up,
So, so, thou common dog, didst thou disgorge
Thy glutton bosom of the royal Richard ;

Lines 36–65 omitted.

Lines 78–85, 'If he
should . . . certain
notice', omitted.

Lines 89–100
omitted.

And now thou wouldst eat thy dead vomit up,
And howl'st to find it.   What trust is in these times ?   100
They that, when Richard liv'd, would have him die
Are now become enamour'd on his grave.
Thou that threw'st dust upon his goodly head,
When through proud London he came sighing on
After th' admired heels of Bolingbroke,   105
Criest now ' O earth, yield us that king again,
And take thou this ! '   O thoughts of men accurs'd !
Past and to come seems best ;   things present, worst.
MOWB. Shall we go draw our numbers, and set on ?
HAST. We are time's subjects, and time bids be gone.   [*Exeunt.*

Lines 89–100 omitted.

Lines 106–108 omitted.

ACT TWO.

SCENE I.   *London.   A street.*

Enter HOSTESS *with two officers,* FANG *and* SNARE.

HOST. Master Fang, have you ent'red the action ?
FANG. It is ent'red.
HOST. Where's your yeoman ?   Is't a lusty yeoman ?   Will 'a stand
to't ?
FANG. Sirrah, where's Snare ?   5
HOST. O Lord, ay !   good Master Snare.
SNARE. Here, here.
FANG. Snare, we must arrest Sir John Falstaff.
HOST. Yea, good Master Snare ;   I have ent'red him and all.
SNARE. It may chance cost some of our lives, for he will stab.
HOST. Alas the day !   take heed of him ;   he stabb'd me in mine own
house, and that most beastly.   In good faith, 'a cares not what
mischief he does, if his weapon be out ;   he will foin like any devil ;
he will spare neither man, woman, nor child.   17
FANG. If I can close with him, I care not for his thrust.
HOST. No, nor I neither ;   I'll be at your elbow.
FANG. An I but fist him once ;   an 'a come but within my vice !   21
HOST. I am undone by his going ;   I warrant you, he's an infinitive
thing upon my score.   Good Master Fang, hold him sure.   Good
Master Snare, let him not scape.   'A comes continuantly to
Pie-corner—saving your manhoods—to buy a saddle ;   and he is
indited to dinner to the Lubber's Head in Lumbert Street, to
Master Smooth's the silkman.   I pray you, since my exion is
ent'red, and my case so openly known to the world, let him be
brought in to his answer.   A hundred mark is a long one for a
poor lone woman to bear ;   and I have borne, and borne, and borne;
and have been fubb'd off, and fubb'd off, and fubb'd off, from
this day to that day, that it is a shame to be thought on.   There
is no honesty in such dealing ;   unless a woman should be made an
ass and a beast, to bear every knave's wrong.   36

Enter SIR JOHN FALSTAFF, Page, *and* BARDOLPH.

Yonder he comes ;   and that arrant malmsey-nose knave, Bardolph,
with him.   Do your offices, do your offices, Master Fang and
Master Snare ;   do me, do me, do me your offices.   39
FAL. How now !   whose mare's dead ?   What's the matter ?

SCENE 6
*Exterior. London.
A Street. Day.*
HOSTESS, FANG.

Lines 3–27, 'Where's your . . . the silkman', omitted.

'and Master Snare' omitted.

FANG. Sir John, I arrest you at the suit of Mistress Quickly.
FAL. Away, varlets! Draw Bardolph. Cut me off the villain's head.
Throw the quean in the channel.   45
HOST. Throw me in the channel! I'll throw thee in the channel.
Wilt thou? wilt thou? thou bastardly rogue! Murder, murder!
Ah, thou honeysuckle villain! wilt thou kill God's officers and the
King's? Ah, thou honey-seed rogue! thou art a honey-seed; | 'Ah, thou honey-seed
a man-queller and a woman-queller.   51 | . . . woman-queller'
  | omitted.
FAL. Keep them off, Bardolph.
FANG. A rescue! a rescue!
HOST. Good people, bring a rescue or two. Thou wot, wot thou! | 'Thou wot . . . thou
thou wot, wot ta? Do, do, thou rogue! do, thou hemp-seed! | hemp-seed' omitted.
PAGE. Away, you scullion! you rampallian! you fustilarian! I'll
tickle your catastrophe.   58

Enter the LORD CHIEF JUSTICE *and his* Men.

CH. JUST. What is the matter? Keep the peace here, ho!
HOST. Good my lord, be good to me. I beseech you, stand to me.
CH. JUST. How now, Sir John! what, are you brawling here?
Doth this become your place, your time, and business?
You should have been well on your way to York.   64
Stand from him, fellow; wherefore hang'st thou upon him? | Line 65 omitted.
HOST. O my most worshipful lord, an't please your Grace, I am a
poor widow of Eastcheap, and he is arrested at my suit.
CH. JUST. For what sum?
HOST. It is more than for some, my lord; it is for all—all I have.
He hath eaten me out of house and home; he hath put all my
substance into that fat belly of his. But I will have some of it out | 'But I will have . . .
again, or I will ride thee a nights like a mare. | ground to get up'
  | omitted.
FAL. I think I am as like to ride the mare, if I have any vantage of
ground to get up.   76
CH. JUST. How comes this, Sir John? Fie! What man of good | 'What man . . . of
temper would endure this tempest of exclamation? Are you not | exclamation'
ashamed to enforce a poor widow to so rough a course to come by | omitted.
her own?   80
FAL. What is the gross sum that I owe thee?
HOST. Marry, if thou wert an honest man, thyself and the money too.
Thou didst swear to me upon a parcel-gilt goblet, sitting in my
Dolphin chamber, at the round table, by a sea-coal fire, upon
Wednesday in Wheeson week, when the Prince broke thy head
for liking his father to a singing-man of Windsor—thou didst
swear to me then, as I was washing thy wound, to marry me and
make me my lady thy wife. Canst thou deny it? Did not | 'Did not goodwife
goodwife Keech, the butcher's wife, come in then and call me | . . . call me madam'
gossip Quickly? Coming in to borrow a mess of vinegar, telling | omitted.
us she had a good dish of prawns, whereby thou didst desire to
eat some, whereby I told thee they were ill for a green wound?
And didst thou not, when she was gone down stairs, desire me to
be no more so familiarity with such poor people, saying that ere
long they should call me madam? And didst thou not kiss me,
and bid me fetch thee thirty shillings? I put thee now to thy
book-oath. Deny it, if thou canst.   99
FAL. My lord, this is a poor mad soul, and she says up and down the
town that her eldest son is like you. She hath been in good case,

and, the truth is, poverty hath distracted her. But for these
foolish officers, I beseech you I may have redress against them.
CH. JUST. Sir John, Sir John, I am well acquainted with your manner
of wrenching the true cause the false way. It is not a confident
brow, nor the throng of words that come with such more than
impudent sauciness from you, can thrust me from a level consideration. You have, as it appears to me, practis'd upon the
easy yielding spirit of this woman, and made her serve your uses
both in purse and in person.   112
HOST. Yea, in truth, my lord.
CH. JUST. Pray thee, peace. Pay her the debt you owe her, and unpay
the villainy you have done with her ; the one you may do with
sterling money, and the other with current repentance.
FAL. My lord, I will not undergo this sneap without reply. You call
honourable boldness impudent sauciness ; if a man will make
curtsy and say nothing, he is virtuous. No, my lord, my humble
duty rememb'red, I will not be your suitor. I say to you I do
desire deliverance from these officers, being upon hasty employment in the King's affairs.   124
CH. JUST. You speak as having power to do wrong ; but answer in
th' effect of your reputation, and satisfy the poor woman.
FAL. Come hither hostess.

Enter GOWER.

CH. JUST. Now, Master Gower, what news ?
GOW. The King, my lord, and Harry Prince of Wales
Are near at hand. The rest the paper tells.   [*Gives a letter.*
FAL. As I am a gentleman !
HOST. Faith, you said so before.
FAL. As I am a gentleman ! Come, no more words of it.   135
HOST. By this heavenly ground I tread on, I must be fain to pawn both
my plate and the tapestry of my dining-chambers.
FAL. Glasses, glasses, is the only drinking ; and for thy walls, a   'Glasses, glasses . . .
pretty slight drollery, or the story of the Prodigal, or the German   fly-bitten tapestries'
hunting, in water-work, is worth a thousand of these bed-hangers   omitted.
and these fly-bitten tapestries. Let it be ten pound, if thou canst.
Come, an 'twere not for thy humours, there's not a better wench
in England. Go, wash thy face, and draw the action. Come,   'Come, thou must
thou must not be in this humour with me ; dost not know me ?   . . . set on to this'
Come, come, I know thou wast set on to this.   147   omitted.
HOST. Pray thee, Sir John, let it be but twenty nobles ; i' faith, I am
loath to pawn my plate, so God save me, la !
FAL. Let it alone ; I'll make other shift. You'll be a fool still.
HOST. Well, you shall have it, though I pawn my gown. I hope
you'll come to supper. You'll pay me all together ?
FAL. Will I live ? [*To* BARDOLPH.] Go, with her, with her   hook on,
hook on.   156
HOST. Will you have Doll Tearsheet meet you at supper ?
FAL. No more words ; let's have her.
                    [*Exeunt* HOSTESS, BARDOLPH, *and* Officers.
CH. JUST. I have heard better news.
FAL. What's the news, my lord ?
CH. JUST. Where lay the King to-night ?
GOW. At Basingstoke, my lord.

FAL. I hope, my lord, all's well.   What is the news, my lord ?   165
CH. JUST. Come all his forces back ?
GOW. No ; fifteen hundred foot, five hundred horse,
    Are march'd up to my Lord of Lancaster,
    Against Northumberland and the Archbishop.
FAL. Comes the King back from Wales, my noble lord ?
CH. JUST. You shall have letters of me presently.   171
    Come, go along with me, good Master Gower.
FAL. My lord !
CH. JUST. What's the matter ?
FAL. Master Gower, shall I entreat you with me to dinner ?
GOW. I must wait upon my good lord here, I thank you, good Sir John.
CH. JUST. Sir John, you loiter here too long, being you are to take
    soldiers up in counties as you go.   180
FAL. Will you sup with me, Master Gower ?
CH. JUST. What foolish master taught you these manners, Sir John ?
FAL. Master Gower, if they become me not, he was a fool that taught
    them me.   This is the right fencing grace, my lord ; tap for tap,
    and so part fair.   186
CH. JUST. Now, the Lord lighten thee ! Thou art a great fool. [Exeunt.

SCENE II. London.   Another street.

Enter PRINCE HENRY and POINS.

PRINCE. Before God, I am exceeding weary.
POINS. Is't come to that ?   I had thought weariness durst not have
    attach'd one of so high blood.
PRINCE. Faith, it does me ; though it discolours the complexion of
    my greatness to acknowledge it.   Doth it not show vilely in me
    to desire small beer ?   6
POINS. Why, a prince should not be so loosely studied as to remember
    so weak a composition.
PRINCE. Belike then my appetite was not princely got ; for, by my
    troth, I do now remember the poor creature, small beer.   But
    indeed these humble considerations make me out of love with
    my greatness.   What a disgrace is it to me to remember thy
    name, or to know thy face to-morrow, or to take note how many
    pair of silk stockings thou hast—viz., these, and those that were
    thy peach-colour'd ones—or to bear the inventory of thy shirts—
    as, one for superfluity, and another for use !   But that the tennis-
    court-keeper knows better than I ; for it is a low ebb of linen with
    thee when thou keepest not racket there ; as thou hast not done a
    great while, because the rest of thy low countries have made a
    shift to eat up thy holland.   And God knows whether those that
    bawl out of the ruins of thy linen shall inherit his kingdom ; but
    the midwives say the children are not in the fault ; whereupon
    the world increases, and kindreds are mightily strengthened.   26
POINS. How ill it follows, after you have laboured so hard, you should
    talk so idly !   Tell me, how many good young princes would do
    so, their fathers being so sick as yours at this time is ?
PRINCE. Shall I tell thee one thing, Poins ?
POINS. Yes, faith ; and let it be an excellent good thing.
PRINCE. It shall serve among wits of no higher breeding than thine.
POINS. Go to ; I stand the push of your one thing that you will tell.

SCENE 7
Interior. London. A
Room in a Tavern.
Day.

'as thou hast not . . .
mightily strength-
ened' omitted.

PRINCE. Marry, I tell thee it is not meet that I should be sad, now
    my father is sick; albeit I could tell to thee—as to one it pleases
    me, for fault of a better, to call my friend—I could be sad and
    sad indeed too.   40
POINS. Very hardly upon such a subject.
PRINCE. By this hand, thou thinkest me as far in the devil's book as
    thou and Falstaff for obduracy and persistency: let the end try
    the man.   But I tell thee my heart bleeds inwardly that my father
    is so sick; and keeping such vile company as thou art hath in
    reason taken from me all ostentation of sorrow.   47
POINS. The reason?
PRINCE. What wouldst thou think of me if I should weep?
POINS. I would think thee a most princely hypocrite.
PRINCE. It would be every man's thought: and thou art a blessed
    fellow to think as every man thinks.   Never a man's thought in
    the world keeps the road-way better than thine.   Every man
    would think me an hypocrite indeed.   And what accites your
    most worshipful thought to think so?   57
POINS. Why, because you have been so lewd and so much engraffed
    to Falstaff.
PRINCE. And to thee.
POINS. By this light, I am well spoke on; I can hear it with mine own
    ears.   The worst that they can say of me is that I am a second
    brother and that I am a proper fellow of my hands; and those
    two things, I confess, I cannot help.   By the mass, here comes | 'By the mass . . .
    Bardolph.   66 | Bardolph' omitted.

Enter BARDOLPH and Page.

PRINCE. And the boy that I gave Falstaff. 'A had him from me | 'And the boy . . . him
    Christian; and look if the fat villain have not transform'd him | ape' omitted.
    ape.
BARD. God save your Grace!
PRINCE. And yours, most noble Bardolph!   71
POINS. Come, you virtuous ass, you bashful fool, must you be blush- | Lines 72–93 omitted.
    ing?   Wherefore blush you now?   What a maidenly man-at-
    arms are you become!   Is't such a matter to get a pottle-pot's
    maidenhead?   75
PAGE. 'A calls me e'en now, my lord, through a red lattice, and I
    could discern no part of his face from the window.   At last I spied
    his eyes; and methought he had made two holes in the alewife's
    new petticoat, and so peep'd through.   80
PRINCE. Has not the boy profited?
BARD. Away, you whoreson upright rabbit, away!
PAGE. Away, you rascally Althæa's dream, away!
PRINCE. Instruct us, boy; what dream, boy?
PAGE. Marry, my lord, Althæa dreamt she was delivered of a fire-
    brand; and therefore I call him her dream.
PRINCE. A crown's worth of good interpretation.   There 'tis, boy.
[Giving a crown.
POINS. O that this blossom could be kept from cankers!   Well, there
    is sixpence to preserve thee.   91
BARD. An you do not make him be hang'd among you, the gallows
    shall have wrong.
PRINCE. And how doth thy master, Bardolph?

BARD. Well, my lord. He heard of your Grace's coming to town.
There's a letter for you.
POINS. Deliver'd with good respect. And how doth the martlemas,
your master?
BARD. In bodily health, sir.   99
POINS. Marry, the immortal part needs a physician; but that moves
not him. Though that be sick, it dies not.
PRINCE. I do allow this wen to be as familiar with me as my dog;
and he holds his place, for look you how he writes.   104
POINS. [*Reads.*] 'John Falstaff, knight'—Every man must know that
as oft as he has occasion to name himself, even like those that are
kin to the King; for they never prick their finger but they say
'There's some of the King's blood spilt'. 'How comes that?'
says he that takes upon him not to conceive. The answer is as
ready as a borrower's cap: 'I am the King's poor cousin, sir'.
PRINCE. Nay, they will be kin to us, or they will fetch it from Japhet.
But the letter: [*Reads.*] 'Sir John Falstaff, knight, to the son of
the King nearest his father, Harry Prince of Wales, greeting'.
POINS. Why, this is a certificate.   116
PRINCE. Peace! [*Reads.*] 'I will imitate the honourable Romans in
brevity.'—
POINS. He sure means brevity in breath, short-winded.
PRINCE. [*Reads.*] 'I commend me to thee, I commend thee, and I
leave thee. Be not too familiar with Poins; for he misuses thy
favours so much that he swears thou art to marry his sister Nell.
Repent at idle times as thou mayst, and so farewell.   123
Thine, by yea and no—which is as much as to say as thou usest
him—JACK FALSTAFF with my familiars, JOHN with my brothers
and sisters, and SIR JOHN with all Europe.'
POINS. My lord, I'll steep this letter in sack and make him eat it.
PRINCE. That's to make him eat twenty of his words. But do you
use me thus, Ned? Must I marry your sister?
POINS. God send the wench no worse fortune! But I never said
so.
PRINCE. Well, thus we play the fools with the time, and the spirits
of the wise sit in the clouds and mock us. Is your master here in
London?   137
BARD. Yea, my lord.
PRINCE. Where sups he? Doth the old boar feed in the old frank?
BARD. At the old place, my lord, in Eastcheap.
PRINCE. What company?
PAGE. Ephesians, my lord, of the old church.
PRINCE. Sup any women with him?   144
PAGE. None, my lord, but old Mistress Quickly and Mistress Doll
Tearsheet.
PRINCE. What pagan may that be?
PAGE. A proper gentlewoman, sir, and a kinswoman of my master's.
PRINCE. Even such kin as the parish heifers are to the town bull.
Shall we steal upon them, Ned, at supper?   152
POINS. I am your shadow, my lord; I'll follow you.
PRINCE. Sirrah, you boy, and Bardolph, no word to your master that
I am yet come to town. There's for your silence.
BARD. I have no tongue, sir.
PAGE. And for mine, sir, I will govern it.

Lines 105–113, 'But
the letter', omitted.

PRINCE. Fare you well ; go. [*Exeunt* BARDOLPH *and* Page.] This
    Doll Tearsheet should be some road.   160
POINS. I warrant you, as common as the way between Saint Albans
    and London.
PRINCE. How might we see Falstaff bestow himself to-night in his
    true colours, and not ourselves be seen ?
POINS. Put on two leathern jerkins and aprons, and wait upon him at
    his table as drawers.   166
PRINCE. From a god to a bull ? A heavy descension ! It was Jove's
    case. From a prince to a prentice ? A low transformation !
    That shall be mine ; for in everything the purpose must weigh
    with the folly. Follow me, Ned.   [*Exeunt.*

SCENE III. *Warkworth. Before the castle.*

Enter NORTHUMBERLAND, LADY NORTHUMBERLAND, *and* LADY PERCY.

SCENE 8
*Interior. A Room in
Warkworth Castle.
Day.*

NORTH. I pray thee, loving wife, and gentle daughter,
    Give even way unto my rough affairs ;
    Put not you on the visage of the times
    And be, like them, to Percy troublesome.
LADY N. I have given over, I will speak no more.   5
    Do what you will ; your wisdom be your guide.
NORTH. Alas, sweet wife, my honour is at pawn ;
    And but my going nothing can redeem it.
LADY P. O, yet, for God's sake, go not to these wars !
    The time was, father, that you broke your word,   10
    When you were more endear'd to it than now ;
    When your own Percy, when my heart's dear Harry,
    Threw many a northward look to see his father
    Bring up his powers ; but he did long in vain.
    Who then persuaded you to stay at home ?   15
    There were two honours lost, yours and your son's.
    For yours, the God of heaven brighten it !
    For his, it stuck upon him as the sun
    In the grey vault of heaven ; and by his light
    Did all the chivalry of England move   20
    To do brave acts. He was indeed the glass
    Wherein the noble youth did dress themselves.
    He had no legs that practis'd not his gait ;
    And speaking thick, which nature made his blemish,
    Became the accents of the valiant ;   25
    For those who could speak low and tardily
    Would turn their own perfection to abuse
    To seem like him : so that in speech, in gait,
    In diet, in affections of delight,
    In military rules, humours of blood,   30
    He was the mark and glass, copy and book,
    That fashion'd others. And him—O wondrous him !
    O miracle of men !—him did you leave—
    Second to none, unseconded by you—
    To look upon the hideous god of war   35
    In disadvantage, to abide a field
    Where nothing but the sound of Hotspur's name
    Did seem defensible. So you left him.

Gordon Gostelow as Bardolph and Bryan Pringle as Pistol

Anthony Quayle as Sir John Falstaff, with Doll Tearsheet (Frances Cuka) and Pistol

Bardolph (Gordon Gostelow) and Mistress Quickly (Brenda Bruce)

Falstaff (Anthony Quayle) with Shallow (Robert Eddison) and Silence (Leslie French)

David Gwillim as Prince Hal tries on the crown beside the dying Henry IV (Jon Finch)

The Lord Chief Justice (Ralph Michael) faces Prince Hal

A group of citizens, including Falstaff (Anthony Quayle), watch King Henry V (David Gwillim) pass in procession

Never, O never, do his ghost the wrong
To hold your honour more precise and nice					40
With others than with him !   Let them alone.
The Marshal and the Archbishop are strong.
Had my sweet Harry had but half their numbers,
To-day might I, hanging on Hotspur's neck,
Have talk'd of Monmouth's grave.
NORTH.						Beshrew your heart,			45
Fair daughter, you do draw my spirits from me
With new lamenting ancient oversights.
But I must go and meet with danger there,
Or it will seek me in another place,
And find me worse provided.
LADY N.					O, fly to Scotland				50
Till that the nobles and the armed commons
Have of their puissance made a little taste.
LADY P. If they get ground and vantage of the King,
Then join you with them, like a rib of steel,
To make strength stronger ; but, for all our loves,			55
First let them try themselves.   So did your son ;
He was so suff'red ; so came I a widow ;
And never shall have length of life enough
To rain upon remembrance with mine eyes,
That it may grow and sprout as high as heaven,			60
For recordation to my noble husband.
NORTH. Come, come, go in with me. 'Tis with my mind		'Come, come, go in
As with the tide swell'd up unto his height,				with me' omitted.
That makes a still-stand, running neither way.
Fain would I go to meet the Archbishop,					65
But many thousand reasons hold me back.
I will resolve for Scotland.   There am I,
Till time and vantage crave my company.		[*Exeunt.*

SCENE IV. *London.   The Boar's Head Tavern in Eastcheap.*

Enter FRANCIS *and another* Drawer.

FRANCIS. What the devil hast thou brought there—apple-johns ?		Lines 1–21 omitted.
Thou knowest Sir John cannot endure an apple-john.
2 DRAW. Mass, thou say'st true. The Prince once set a dish of
apple-johns before him, and told him there were five more Sir
Johns ; and, putting off his hat, said ' I will now take my leave of
these six dry, round, old, withered knights '.   It ang'red him to
the heart ; but he hath forgot that.						9
FRANCIS. Why, then, cover and set them down ; and see if thou
canst find out Sneak's noise ; Mistress Tearsheet would fain
hear some music.

Enter third Drawer.

3 DRAW. Dispatch !   The room where they supp'd is too hot ; they'll
come in straight.								14
FRANCIS. Sirrah, here will be the Prince and Master Poins anon ;
and they will put on two of our jerkins and aprons ; and Sir John
must not know of it.   Bardolph hath brought word.

3 DRAW. By the mass, here will be old utis ; it will be an excellent stratagem.   20
2 DRAW. I'll see if I can find out Sneak.

[Exeunt second and third Drawers.

Enter Hostess *and* DOLL TEARSHEET.

HOST. I'faith, sweetheart, methinks now you are in an excellent good temperality.   Your pulsidge beats as extraordinarily as heart would desire ; and your colour, I warrant you, is as red as any rose, in good truth, la !   But, i' faith, you have drunk too much canaries ; and that's a marvellous searching wine, and it perfumes the blood ere one can say ' What's this ? '   How do you now ?
DOLL. Better than I was—hem.   30
HOST. Why, that's well said ; a good heart's worth gold.   Lo, here comes Sir John.

Enter FALSTAFF.

FAL. [*Singing.*] ' When Arthur first in court '—Empty the jordan. [*Exit* FRANCIS.]—[*Singing.*] ' And was a worthy king '—How now, Mistress Doll !   35
HOST. Sick of a calm ; yea, good faith.
FAL. So is all her sect ; an they be once in a calm, they are sick.
DOLL. A pox damn you, you muddy rascal !   Is that all the comfort you give me ?   40
FAL. You make fat rascals, Mistress Doll.
DOLL. I make them !   Gluttony and diseases make them :   I make them not.
FAL. If the cook help to make the gluttony, you help to make the diseases, Doll.   We catch of you, Doll, we catch of you ; grant that, my poor virtue, grant that.   46
DOLL. Yea, joy, our chains and our jewels.
FAL. ' Your brooches, pearls, and ouches.'   For to serve bravely is to come halting off ; you know, to come off the breach with his pike bent bravely, and to surgery bravely ; to venture upon the charg'd chambers bravely—   51
DOLL. Hang yourself, you muddy conger, hang yourself !
HOST. By my troth, this is the old fashion ; you two never meet but you fall to some discord.   You are both, i' good truth, as rheumatic as two dry toasts ; you cannot one bear with another's confirmities.   What the good-year !   one must bear, and that must be you.   You are the weaker vessel, as they say, the emptier vessel.   58
DOLL. Can a weak empty vessel bear such a huge full hogshead ? There's a whole merchant's venture of Bourdeaux stuff in him ; you have not seen a hulk better stuff'd in the hold.   Come, I'll be friends with thee, Jack.   Thou art going to the wars ; and whether I shall ever see thee again or no, there is nobody cares.64

Re-enter FRANCIS.

FRANCIS. Sir, Ancient Pistol's below and would speak with you.
DOLL. Hang him, swaggering rascal !   Let him not come hither ; it is the foul-mouth'dst rogue in England.
HOST. If he swagger, let him not come here.   No, by my faith !   I must live among my neighbours ; I'll no swaggerers.   I am in good name and fame with the very best.   Shut the door.   There

Lines 1–21 omitted.

SCENE 9
Interior. Eastcheap.
The Boar's Head
Tavern. Day.
HOSTESS, DOLL
TEARSHEET

Exit the Drawer.

Lines 47–51 omitted.

BARDOLPH enters.

BARDOLPH for
Francis.

comes no swaggerers here ; I have not liv'd all this while to have
swaggering now. Shut the door, I pray you.

FAL. Dost thou hear, hostess ?   75

HOST. Pray ye, pacify yourself, Sir John ; there comes no swaggerers
here.

FAL. Dost thou hear ?   It is mine ancient.

HOST. Tilly-fally, Sir John, ne'er tell me ; and your ancient swagg'rer
comes not in my doors.   I was before Master Tisick, the debuty,
t' other day ; and, as he said to me—'twas no longer ago than
Wednesday last, i' good faith !—' Neighbour Quickly,' says he—
Master Dumbe, our minister, was by then—' Neighbour Quickly,'
says he ' receive those that are civil, for ' said he ' you are in an ill
name.'   Now 'a said so, I can tell whereupon.   ' For ' says he
' you are an honest woman and well thought on, therefore take
heed what guests you receive.   Receive ' says he ' no swaggering
companions.'   There comes none here.   You would bless you to
hear what he said.   No, I'll no swagg'rers.   91

FAL. He's no swagg'rer, hostess ; a tame cheater, i' faith ; you may
stroke him as gently as a puppy greyhound.   He'll not swagger
with a Barbary hen, if her feathers turn back in any show of
resistance.   Call him up, drawer.   [*Exit* FRANCIS.

HOST. Cheater, call you him ?   I will bar no honest man my house,
nor no cheater ; but I do not love swaggering, by my troth.   I am
the worse when one says ' swagger '.   Feel, masters, how I shake ;
look you, I warrant you.   100

DOLL. So you do, hostess.

HOST. Do I ?   Yea, in very truth, do I, an 'twere an aspen leaf.   I
cannot abide swagg'rers.

Enter PISTOL, BARDOLPH, *and* PAGE.

PIST. God save you, Sir John !   104

FAL. Welcome, Ancient Pistol.   Here, Pistol, I charge you with a
cup of sack ; do you discharge upon mine hostess.

PIST. I will discharge upon her, Sir John, with two bullets.

FAL. She is pistol-proof, sir ; you shall not hardly offend her.

HOST. Come, I'll drink no proofs nor no bullets.   I'll drink no more
than will do me good, for no man's pleasure, I.   113

PIST. Then to you, Mistress Dorothy ; I will charge you.

DOLL. Charge me !   I scorn you, scurvy companion.   What !   you
poor, base, rascally, cheating, lack-linen mate !   Away,   you
mouldy rogue, away !   I am meat for your master.

PIST. I know you, Mistress Dorothy.   119

DOLL. Away, you cut-purse rascal !   you filthy bung, away !   By this
wine, I'll thrust my knife in your mouldy chaps, an you play the
saucy cuttle with me.   Away, you bottle-ale rascal !   you basket-
hilt stale juggler, you !   Since when, I pray you sir ?   God's
light, with two points on your shoulder ?   Much !   125

PIST. God let me not live but I will murder your ruff for this.

FAL. No more, Pistol ; I would not have you go off here.   Discharge
yourself of our company, Pistol.

HOST. No, good Captain Pistol ; not here, sweet captain.

DOLL. Captain !   Thou abominable damn'd cheater, art thou not
ashamed to be called captain ?   An captains were of my mind,
they would truncheon you out, for taking their names upon you

'He'll not swagger
. . . resistance'
omitted. For 'drawer'
read 'Bardolph'. *Exit*
BARDOLPH.

before you have earn'd them. You a captain! you slave, for
what? For tearing a poor whore's ruff in a bawdy-house? He a
captain! hang him, rogue! He lives upon mouldy stew'd
prunes and dried cakes. A captain! God's light, these villains
will make the word as odious as the word ' occupy '; which was
an excellent good word before it was ill sorted. Therefore
captains had need look to't.   141

BARD. Pray thee go down, good ancient.

FAL. Hark thee hither, Mistress Doll.

PIST. Not I! I tell thee what, Corporal Bardolph, I could tear her;
I'll be reveng'd of her.

PAGE. Pray thee go down.

PIST. I'll see her damn'd first; to Pluto's damn'd lake, by this hand,
to th' infernal deep, with Erebus and tortures vile also. Hold
hook and line, say I. Down, down, dogs! down, faitors! Have
we not Hiren here?   151

HOST. Good Captain Peesel, be quiet; 'tis very late, i' faith; I beseek
you now, aggravate your choler.

PIST. These be good humours, indeed! Shall packhorses,
And hollow pamper'd jades of Asia,   155
Which cannot go but thirty mile a day,
Compare with Cæsars, and with Cannibals,
And Troiant Greeks? Nay, rather damn them with
King Cerberus; and let the welkin roar.
Shall we fall foul for toys?   160

HOST. By my troth, Captain, these are very bitter words.

BARD. Be gone, good ancient; this will grow to a brawl anon.

PIST. Die men like dogs! Give crowns like pins! Have we not
Hiren here?   165

HOST. O' my word, Captain, there's none such here. What the
good-year! do you think I would deny her? For God's sake,
be quiet.

PIST. Then feed and be fat, my fair Calipolis.
Come, give's some sack.   170
' Si fortune me tormente sperato me contento.'
Fear we broadsides? No, let the fiend give fire.
Give me some sack; and, sweetheart, lie thou there.
                              [*Laying down his sword.*
Come we to full points here, and are etceteras nothings?

FAL. Pistol, I would be quiet.   175

PIST. Sweet knight, I kiss thy neaf. What! we have seen the seven
stars.

DOLL. For God's sake thrust him down stairs; I cannot endure such
a fustian rascal.

PIST. Thrust him down stairs! Know we not Galloway nags?

FAL. Quoit him down, Bardolph, like a shove-groat shilling. Nay,
an 'a do nothing but speak nothing, 'a shall be nothing here.

BARD. Come, get you down stairs.   185

PIST. What! shall we have incision? Shall we imbrue?
                              [*Snatching up his sword.*
Then death rock me asleep, abridge my doleful days!
Why, then, let grievous, ghastly, gaping wounds
Untwine the Sisters Three! Come, Atropos, I say!

HOST. Here's goodly stuff toward!   190

Marginal notes:

'God's light . . . ill sorted' omitted.

Line 142 omitted.
After line 143, add:
BARD. Good ancient, downstairs, good ancient.
Lines 146–151 omitted.

'Be gone . . . be quiet' omitted.

After line 171, add:
BARD. Pray thee go down, good ancient.

'Know we not Galloway nags?' omitted.
'Nay, an 'a do . . . down stairs' omitted.
After line 185, add:
BARD. This will grow to a brawl anon, pray you downstairs.

FAL. Give me my rapier, boy.
DOLL. I pray thee, Jack, I pray thee, do not draw.
FAL. Get you down stairs.   [*Drawing and driving* PISTOL *out.*
HOST. Here's a goodly tumult! I'll forswear keeping house afore I'll
 be in these tirrits and frights. So; murder, I warrant now.
 Alas, alas! put up your naked weapons, put up your naked
 weapons.   [*Exeunt* PISTOL *and* BARDOLPH.
DOLL. I pray thee, Jack, be quiet; the rascal's gone. Ah, you
 whoreson little valiant villain, you!
HOST. Are you not hurt i' th' groin? Methought 'a made a shrewd
 thrust at your belly.   201

Re-enter BARDOLPH.

FAL. Have you turn'd him out a doors?
BARD. Yea, sir. The rascal's drunk. You have hurt him, sir, i' th'
 shoulder.
FAL. A rascal! to brave me!   205
DOLL. Ah, you sweet little rogue, you! Alas, poor ape, how thou
 sweat'st! Come, let me wipe thy face. Come on, you whoreson
 chops. Ah, rogue! i' faith, I love thee. Thou art as valorous
 as Hector of Troy, worth five of Agamemnon, and ten times better
 than the Nine Worthies. Ah, villain!   211
FAL. A rascally slave! I will toss the rogue in a blanket.
DOLL. Do, an thou dar'st for thy heart. An thou dost, I'll canvass
 thee between a pair of sheets.

Enter MUSICIANS.

PAGE. The music is come, sir.
FAL. Let them play. Play, sirs. Sit on my knee, Doll. A rascal
 bragging slave! The rogue fled from me like quicksilver.
DOLL. I' faith, and thou follow'dst him like a church. Thou whoreson
 little tidy Bartholomew boar-pig, when wilt thou leave fighting
 a days and foining a nights, and begin to patch up thine old body
 for heaven?

Enter, behind, PRINCE HENRY *and* POINS *disguised as* drawers.

FAL. Peace, good Doll! Do not speak like a death's-head; do not
 bid me remember mine end.   225
DOLL. Sirrah, what humour 's the Prince of?
FAL. A good shallow young fellow. 'A would have made a good
 pantler; 'a would ha' chipp'd bread well.
DOLL. They say Poins has a good wit.
FAL. He a good wit! hang him, baboon! His wit's as thick as
 Tewksbury mustard; there's no more conceit in him than is in a
 mallet.   232
DOLL. Why does the Prince love him so, then?
FAL. Because their legs are both of a bigness, and 'a plays at quoits
 well, and eats conger and fennel, and drinks off candles' ends for
 flap-dragons, and rides the wild mare with the boys, and jumps
 upon join'd-stools, and swears with a good grace, and wears his
 boots very smooth, like unto the sign of the Leg, and breeds no
 bate with telling of discreet stories; and such other gambol
 faculties 'a has, that show a weak mind and an able body, for the
 which the Prince admits him. For the Prince himself is such

Right margin notes:

In the television production the Musicians are PRINCE HENRY and POINS in disguise.

See above.

'there's no more . . . mallet' omitted.

'and eats conger . . . join'd-stools' omitted.
'and wears . . . discreet stories' omitted.
'for the which the Prince admits him' omitted.

another ; the weight of a hair will turn the scales between their
avoirdupois.   244
PRINCE. Would not this nave of a wheel have his ears cut off ?
POINS. Let's beat him before his whore.
PRINCE. Look whe'er the wither'd elder hath not his poll claw'd like
a parrot.
POINS. Is it not strange that desire should so many years outlive
performance ?
FAL. Kiss me, Doll.
PRINCE. Saturn and Venus this year in conjunction ! What says th'
almanac to that ?   254
POINS. And look whether the fiery Trigon, his man, be not lisping to | 'And look . . .
his master's old tables, his note-book, his counsel-keeper. | counsel-keeper'
FAL. Thou dost give me flattering busses. | omitted.
DOLL. By my troth, I kiss thee with a most constant heart.   260
FAL. I am old, I am old.
DOLL. I love thee better than I love e'er a scurvy young boy of them
all.
FAL. What stuff wilt have a kirtle of ? I shall receive money a
Thursday. Shalt have a cap to-morrow. A merry song, come.
'A grows late ; we'll to bed. Thou't forget me when I am gone.
DOLL. By my troth, thou't set me a-weeping, an thou say'st so.
Prove that ever I dress myself handsome till thy return. Well,
hearken a' th' end.   270
FAL. Some sack, Francis.
PRINCE. ⎫
POINS. ⎬ Anon, anon, sir.   [Advancing.
FAL. Ha ! a bastard son of the King's ? And art thou not Poins his
brother ?
PRINCE. Why, thou globe of sinful continents, what a life dost thou
lead !   276
FAL. A better than thou. I am a gentleman : thou art a drawer.
PRINCE. Very true, sir, and I come to draw you out by the ears.
HOST. O, the Lord preserve thy Grace ! By my troth, welcome to | HOSTESS and
London. Now the Lord bless that sweet face of thine ! O Jesu, | BARDOLPH enter.
are you come from Wales ?   283 | 'O, the Lord . . . to
FAL. Thou whoreson mad compound of majesty, by this light flesh | London' omitted.
and corrupt blood, thou art welcome. [Leaning his hand upon DOLL.
DOLL. How, you fat fool ! I scorn you.
POINS. My lord, he will drive you out of your revenge and turn all
to a merriment, if you take not the heat.
PRINCE. You whoreson candle-mine, you, how vilely did you speak
of me even now before this honest, virtuous, civil gentlewoman !
HOST. God's blessing of your good heart ! and so she is, by my troth.
FAL. Didst thou hear me ?
PRINCE. Yea ; and you knew me, as you did when you ran away by
Gadshill. You knew I was at your back, and spoke it on purpose
to try my patience.   297
FAL. No, no, no ; not so ; I did not think thou wast within hearing.
PRINCE. I shall drive you then to confess the wilful abuse, and then
I know how to handle you.
FAL. No abuse, Hal, o' mine honour ; no abuse.
PRINCE. Not—to dispraise me, and call me pantler, and bread-chipper,
and I know not what !

Anthony Quayle as Falstaff and Frances Cuka as Doll Tearsheet

FAL. No abuse, Hal.   305
POINS. No abuse!
FAL. No abuse, Ned, i' th' world; honest Ned, none. I disprais'd
  him before the wicked—that the wicked might not fall in love with
  thee; in which doing, I have done the part of a careful friend
  and a true subject; and thy father is to give me thanks for it. No
  abuse, Hal; none, Ned, none; no, faith, boys, none.   312
PRINCE. See now, whether pure fear and entire cowardice doth not
  make thee wrong this virtuous gentlewoman to close with us?
  Is she of the wicked? Is thine hostess here of the wicked? Or
  is thy boy of the wicked? Or honest Bardolph, whose zeal burns
  in his nose, of the wicked?
POINS. Answer, thou dead elm, answer.   319
FAL. The fiend hath prick'd down Bardolph irrecoverable; and his
  face is Lucifer's privy-kitchen, where he doth nothing but roast
  malt-worms. For the boy—there is a good angel about him;
  but the devil outbids him too.
PRINCE. For the women?   325
FAL. For one of them—she's in hell already, and burns poor souls.
  For th' other—I owe her money; and whether she be damn'd for
  that, I know not.
HOST. No, I warrant you.   329
FAL. No, I think thou art not; I think thou art quit for that. Marry, | Lines 330–338
  there is another indictment upon thee for suffering flesh to be | omitted.
  eaten in thy house, contrary to the law; for the which I think
  thou wilt howl.
HOST. All vict'lers do so. What's a joint of mutton or two in a whole
  Lent?   335
PRINCE. You, gentlewoman—
DOLL. What says your Grace?
FAL. His Grace says that which his flesh rebels against.
                                        [Knocking within.
| HOST. Who knocks so loud at door? Look to th' door there, Francis. | 'Look to . . . Francis'
                                                                         omitted.
                        Enter PETO.

PRINCE. Peto, how now! What news?   341
PET. The King your father is at Westminster;
  And there are twenty weak and wearied posts
  Come from the north; and as I came along
  I met and overtook a dozen captains,   345
  Bare-headed, sweating, knocking at the taverns,
  And asking every one for Sir John Falstaff.
PRINCE. By heaven, Poins, I feel me much to blame
  So idly to profane the precious time,
  When tempest of commotion, like the south,   350 | Lines 350–352
  Borne with black vapour, doth begin to melt | omitted.
  And drop upon our bare unarmed heads.
  Give me my sword and cloak. Falstaff, good night.
                  [*Exeunt* PRINCE, POINS, PETO, *and* BARDOLPH.
FAL. Now comes in the sweetest morsel of the night, and we must
  hence, and leave it unpick'd. [*Knocking within.*] More knocking
  at the door!   356
                  Re-enter BARDOLPH.

How now ! What's the matter ?
BARD. You must away to court, sir, presently ;
A dozen captains stay at door for you.
FAL. [*To the* PAGE.] Pay the musicians, sirrah.—Farewell, hostess ; | Stage direction and
farewell, Doll. You see, my good wenches, how men of merit   'Pay the musicians,
are sought after ; the undeserver may sleep, when the man of   sirrah' omitted.
action is call'd on. Farewell, good wenches. If I be not sent
away post, I will see you again ere I go.   365
DOLL. I cannot speak. If my heart be not ready to burst ! Well,
sweet Jack, have a care of thyself.
FAL. Farewell, farewell.
                      [*Exeunt* FALSTAFF *and* BARDOLPH.
HOST. Well, fare thee well. I have known thee these twenty-nine
years, come peascod-time ; but an honester and truer-hearted
man—well, fare thee well.   371
BARD. [*Within.*] Mistress Tearsheet ! | Lines 372–376
HOST. What's the matter ?   omitted.
BARD. [*Within.*] Bid Mistress Tearsheet come to my master.
HOST. O, run Doll, run, run, good Doll.Come. [*To* BARDOLPH.] She
comes blubber'd.—Yea, will you come, Doll ?   [*Exeunt.

ACT THREE.

SCENE I. *Westminster. The palace.*   SCENE 10
                                                                 Interior. Palace of
Enter the KING *in his nightgown, with a* Page.   *Westminster. The*
                                                                 King's Bedroom.
                                                                 Night.
KING. Go call the Earls of Surrey and of Warwick ;   The KING alone.
But, ere they come, bid them o'er-read these letters
And well consider of them. Make good speed.   [*Exit* Page. | Lines 1–3 omitted.
How many thousands of my poorest subjects
Are at this hour asleep ! O sleep, O gentle sleep,   5
Nature's soft nurse, how have I frighted thee,
That thou no more wilt weigh my eyelids down,
And steep my senses in forgetfulness ?
Why rather, sleep, liest thou in smoky cribs,
Upon uneasy pallets stretching thee,   10
And hush'd with buzzing night-flies to thy slumber,
Than in the perfum'd chambers of the great,
Under the canopies of costly state,
And lull'd with sound of sweetest melody ?
O thou dull god, why liest thou with the vile   15
In loathsome beds, and leav'st the kingly couch
A watch-case or a common 'larum-bell ?
Wilt thou upon the high and giddy mast
Seal up the ship-boy's eyes, and rock his brains
In cradle of the rude imperious surge,   20
And in the visitation of the winds,
Who take the ruffian billows by the top,
Curling their monstrous heads, and hanging them
With deafing clamour in the slippery clouds,
That with the hurly death itself awakes ?   25
Canst thou, O partial sleep, give thy repose
To the wet sea-boy in an hour so rude ;
And in the calmest and most stillest night,

57

With all appliances and means to boot,
Deny it to a king ?   Then, happy low, lie down !   30
Uneasy lies the head that wears a crown.

Enter WARWICK *and* SURREY.

WAR. Many good morrows to your Majesty !
KING. Is it good morrow, lords ?
WAR. 'Tis one o'clock, and past.
KING. Why then, good morrow to you all, my lords.   35
Have you read o'er the letters that I sent you ?
WAR. We have, my liege.
KING. Then you perceive the body of our kingdom
How foul it is ;   what rank diseases grow,
And with what danger, near the heart of it.   40
WAR. It is but as a body yet distempered ;
Which to his former strength may be restored
With good advice and little medicine.
My Lord Northumberland will soon be cool'd.
KING. O God ! that one might read the book of fate, 45
And see the revolution of the times
Make mountains level, and the continent,
Weary of solid firmness, melt itself
Into the sea ;   and other times to see
The beachy girdle of the ocean   50
Too wide for Neptune's hips ;   how chances mock,
And changes fill the cup of alteration
With divers liquors !   O, if this were seen,
The happiest youth, viewing his progress through,
What perils past, what crosses to ensue,   55
Would shut the book and sit him down and die.
'Tis not ten years gone
Since Richard and Northumberland, great friends,
Did feast together, and in two years after
Were they at wars.   It is but eight years since   60
This Percy was the man nearest my soul ;
Who like a brother toil'd in my affairs
And laid his love and life under my foot ;
Yea, for my sake, even to the eyes of Richard
Gave him defiance.   But which of you was by—   65
[*To Warwick.*]   You, cousin Nevil, as I may remember—
When Richard, with his eye brim full of tears,
Then check'd and rated by Northumberland,
Did speak these words, now prov'd a prophecy ?
' Northumberland, thou ladder by the which   70
My cousin Bolingbroke ascends my throne '—
Though then, God knows, I had no such intent
But that necessity so bow'd the state
That I and greatness were compell'd to kiss—
' The time shall come '—thus did he follow it—   75
' The time will come that foul sin, gathering head,
Shall break into corruption ' so went on,
Foretelling this same time's condition
And the division of our amity.
WAR. There is a history in all men's lives,   80

Figuring the natures of the times deceas'd ;
The which observ'd, a man may prophesy,
With a near aim, of the main chance of things
As yet not come to life, who in their seeds
And weak beginning lie intreasured.   85
Such things become the hatch and brood of time ;
And, by the necessary form of this,
King Richard might create a perfect guess
That great Northumberland, then false to him,
Would of that seed grow to a greater falseness ;   90
Which should not find a ground to root upon
Unless on you.
KING. Are these things then necessities ?
Then let us meet them like necessities ;
And that same word even now cries out on us.
They say the Bishop and Northumberland   95
Are fifty thousand strong.
WAR.   It cannot be, my lord.
Rumour doth double, like the voice and echo,
The numbers of the feared.   Please it your Grace
To go to bed.   Upon my soul, my lord,
The powers that you already have sent forth   100
Shall bring this prize in very easily.
To comfort you the more, I have receiv'd
A certain instance that Glendower is dead.
Your Majesty hath been this fortnight ill ;
And these unseasoned hours perforce must add   105
Unto your sickness.
KING.   I will take your counsel.
And, were these inward wars once out of hand,
We would, dear lords, unto the Holy Land.   [*Exeunt.*

SCENE II. *Gloucestershire. Before Justice Shallow's house.*

Enter SHALLOW *and* SILENCE, *meeting ;* MOULDY, SHADOW, WART,
     FEEBLE, BULLCALF, *and* Servants *behind.*

SHAL. Come on, come on, come on ; give me your hand, sir ; give
    me your hand, sir.   An early stirrer, by the rood !   And how
    doth my good cousin Silence ?
SIL. Good morrow, good cousin Shallow.   4
SHAL. And how doth my cousin, your bed-fellow ? and your fairest
    daughter and mine, my god-daughter Ellen ?
SIL. Alas, a black ousel, cousin Shallow !
SHAL. By yea and no, sir.   I dare say my cousin William is become
    a good scholar ; he is at Oxford still, is he not ?   10
SIL. Indeed, sir, to my cost.
SHAL. 'A must, then, to the Inns o' Court shortly.   I was once of
    Clement's Inn ; where I think they will talk of mad Shallow yet.
SIL. You were call'd ' lusty Shallow ' then, cousin.   15
SHAL. By the mass, I was call'd anything ; and I would have done
    anything indeed too, and roundly too.   There was I, and little
    John Doit of Staffordshire, and black George Barnes, and Francis
    Pickbone, and Will Squele a Cotsole man—you had not four such
    swinge-bucklers in all the Inns of Court again.   And I may say

to you we knew where the bona-robas were, and had the best of
them all at commandment. Then was Jack Falstaff, now Sir
John, a boy, and page to Thomas Mowbray, Duke of Norfolk. 25
SIL. This Sir John, cousin, that comes hither anon about soldiers?
SHAL. The same Sir John, the very same. I see him break Scoggin's
head at the court gate, when 'a was a crack not thus high; and
the very same day did I fight with one Sampson Stockfish, a
fruiterer, behind Gray's Inn. Jesu, Jesu, the mad days that I
have spent! and to see how many of my old acquaintance are dead!
SIL. We shall all follow, cousin.   34
SHAL. Certain, 'tis certain; very sure, very sure. Death, as the
Psalmist saith, is certain to all; all shall die. How a good yoke
of bullocks at Stamford fair?
SIL. By my troth, I was not there.
SHAL. Death is certain. Is old Double of your town living yet? 40
SIL. Dead, sir.
SHAL. Jesu, Jesu, dead! 'A drew a good bow; and dead! 'A shot
a fine shoot. John a Gaunt loved him well, and betted much
money on his head. Dead! 'A would have clapp'd i' th' clout
at twelve score, and carried you a forehand shaft a fourteen and
fourteen and a half, that it would have done a man's heart good
to see. How a score of ewes now?
SIL. Thereafter as they be—a score of good ewes may be worth ten
pounds.   50
SHAL. And is old Double dead?

               Enter BARDOLPH *and* One *with him.*

SIL. Here come two of Sir John Falstaff's men, as I think.
SHAL. Good morrow, honest gentlemen.
BARD. I beseech you, which is Justice Shallow?   55
SHAL. I am Robert Shallow, sir, a poor esquire of this county, and
one of the King's justices of the peace. What is your good
pleasure with me?
BARD. My captain, sir, commends him to you; my captain, Sir John
Falstaff—a tall gentleman, by heaven, and a most gallant leader.
SHAL. He greets me well, sir; I knew him a good backsword man.
How doth the good knight? May I ask how my lady his wife
doth?   64
BARD. Sir, pardon; a soldier is better accommodated than with a
wife.
SHAL. It is well said, in faith, sir; and it is well said indeed too.
'Better accommodated'! It is good; yea, indeed, is it. Good
phrases are surely, and ever were very commendable. 'Accommodated'! It comes of accommodo. Very good; a good phrase.
BARD. Pardon, sir; I have heard the word. 'Phrase' call you it?
By this day, I know not the phrase; but I will maintain the word
with my sword to be a soldier-like word, and a word of exceeding
good command, by heaven. Accommodated: that is, when a
man is, as they say, accommodated; or, when a man is being—
whereby 'a may be thought to be accommodated; which is an
excellent thing.   79

               Enter FALSTAFF.

SHAL. It is very just. Look, here comes good Sir John. Give me

Right margin notes:

Enter BARDOLPH
alone.

BARDOLPH for
SHALLOW.

'Accommodated . . .
excellent thing'
omitted.

'It is very just'
omitted.

your good hand, give me your worship's good hand. By my
troth, you like well and bear your years very well. Welcome,
good Sir John.   84
FAL. I am glad to see you well, good Master Robert Shallow. Master
   Surecard, as I think?
SHAL. No, Sir John; it is my cousin Silence, in commission with me.
FAL. Good Master Silence, it well befits you should be of the
   peace.
SIL. Your good worship is welcome.
FAL. Fie! this is hot weather. Gentlemen, have you provided me
   here half a dozen sufficient men?
SHAL. Marry, have we, sir. Will you sit?
FAL. Let me see them, I beseech you.   95
SHAL. Where's the roll? Where's the roll? Where's the roll?
   Let me see, let me see, let me see. So, so, so, so, so—so, so—yea,
   marry, sir. Rafe Mouldy! Let them appear as I call; let them
   do so, let them do so. Let me see; where is Mouldy?
MOUL. Here, an't please you.
SHAL. What think you, Sir John? A good limb'd fellow; young,
   strong, and of good friends.
FAL. Is thy name Mouldy?
MOUL. Yea, an't please you.   105
FAL. 'Tis the more time thou wert us'd.
SHAL. Ha, ha, ha! most excellent, i' faith! Things that are mouldy
   lack use. Very singular good! In faith, well said, Sir John;
   very well said.
FAL. Prick him.   110
MOUL. I was prick'd well enough before, an you could have let me
   alone. My old dame will be undone now for one to do her
   husbandry and her drudgery. You need not to have prick'd me;
   there are other men fitter to go out than I.   115
FAL. Go to; peace, Mouldy; you shall go. Mouldy, it is time you
   were spent.
MOUL. Spent!
SHAL. Peace, fellow, peace; stand aside; know you where you are?
   For th' other, Sir John—let me see. Simon Shadow!
FAL. Yea, marry, let me have him to sit under. He's like to be a cold | 'Yea, marry' omitted.
   soldier.
SHAL. Where's Shadow?
SHAD. Here, sir.   125
FAL. Shadow, whose son art thou?
SHAD. My mother's son, sir.
FAL. Thy mother's son! Like enough; and thy father's shadow.
   So the son of the female is the shadow of the male. It is often so | 'So the son . . .
   indeed; but much of the father's substance!   131 | substance' omitted.
SHAL. Do you like him, Sir John?
FAL. Shadow will serve for summer. Prick him; for we have a | 'for we have . . .
   number of shadows fill up the muster-book. | muster-book'
SHAL. Thomas Wart! | omitted.
FAL. Where's he?
WART. Here, sir.
FAL. Is thy name Wart?
WART. Yea, sir.
FAL. Thou art a very ragged wart.   140

SHAL. Shall I prick him, Sir John?

FAL. It were superfluous; for his apparel is built upon his back, and the whole frame stands upon pins. Prick him no more.

SHAL. Ha, ha, ha! You can do it, sir; you can do it. I commend you well. Francis Feeble!   146

FEE. Here, sir.

FAL. What trade art thou, Feeble?

FEE. A woman's tailor, sir.

SHAL. Shall I prick him, sir?

FAL. You may; but if he had been a man's tailor, he'd ha' prick'd you. Wilt thou make as many holes in an enemy's battle as thou hast done in a woman's petticoat?   154

FEE. I will do my good will, sir; you can have no more.

FAL. Well said, good woman's tailor! well said, courageous Feeble! Thou wilt be as valiant as the wrathful dove or most magnanimous mouse. Prick the woman's tailor—well, Master Shallow, deep, Master Shallow.

FEE. I would Wart might have gone, sir.   160

FAL. I would thou wert a man's tailor, that thou mightst mend him and make him fit to go. I cannot put him to a private soldier, that is the leader of so many thousands. Let that suffice, most forcible Feeble.

FEE. It shall suffice, sir.

FAL. I am bound to thee, reverend Feeble. Who is next?

SHAL. Peter Bullcalf o' th' green!

FAL. Yea, marry, let's see Bullcalf.

BULL. Here, sir.   170

FAL. Fore God, a likely fellow! Come, prick me Bullcalf till he roar again.

BULL. O Lord! good my lord captain—

FAL. What, dost thou roar before thou art prick'd?

BULL. O Lord, sir! I am a diseased man.

FAL. What disease hast thou?

BULL. A whoreson cold, sir, a cough, sir, which I caught with ringing in the King's affairs upon his coronation day, sir.   179

FAL. Come, thou shalt go to the wars in a gown. We will have away thy cold; and I will take such order that thy friends shall ring for thee. Is here all?

SHAL. Here is two more call'd than your number. You must have but four here, sir; and so, I pray you, go in with me to dinner.

FAL. Come, I will go drink with you, but I cannot tarry dinner. I am glad to see you, by my troth, Master Shallow.

SHAL. O, Sir John, do you remember since we lay all night in the windmill in Saint George's Field?   190

FAL. No more of that, Master Shallow, no more of that.

SHAL. Ha, 'twas a merry night. And is Jane Nightwork alive?

FAL. She lives, Master Shallow.

SHAL. She never could away with me.

FAL. Never, never; she would always say she could not abide Master Shallow.

SHAL. By the mass, I could anger her to th' heart. She was then a bona-roba. Doth she hold her own well?

FAL. Old, old, Master Shallow.   201

'I would Wart . . .
reverend Feeble'
omitted.

SHAL. Nay, she must be old; she cannot choose but be old; certain
 she's old; and had Robin Nightwork, by old Nightwork, before
 I came to Clement's Inn.
SIL. That's fifty-five year ago.
SHAL. Ha, cousin Silence, that thou hadst seen that that this knight
 and I have seen! Ha, Sir John, said I well?
FAL. We have heard the chimes at midnight, Master Shallow.   210
SHAL. That we have, that we have, that we have; in faith, Sir John,
 we have. Our watchword was 'Hem, boys!' Come, let's to
 dinner; come, let's to dinner. Jesus, the days that we have
 seen! Come, come.   [*Exeunt* FALSTAFF *and the* Justices.
BULL. Good Master Corporate Bardolph, stand my friend; and here's
 four Harry ten shillings in French crowns for you. In very
 truth, sir, I had as lief be hang'd, sir, as go. And yet, for mine
 own part, sir, I do not care; but rather because I am unwilling
 and, for mine own part, have a desire to stay with my friends;
 else, sir, I did not care for mine own part so much.   221
BARD. Go to; stand aside.
MOUL. And, good Master Corporal Captain, for my old dame's sake,
 stand my friend. She has nobody to do anything about her when
 I am gone; and she is old, and cannot help herself. You shall
 have forty, sir.
BARD. Go to; stand aside.
FEE. By my troth, I care not; a man can die but once; we owe God
 a death. I'll ne'er bear a base mind. An't be my destiny, so;
 an't be not, so. No man's too good to serve's Prince; and, let it
 go which way it will, he that dies this year is quit for the next. 232
BARD. Well said; th'art a good fellow.
FEE. Faith, I'll bear no base mind.

Re-enter FALSTAFF *and the* Justices.

FAL. Come, sir, which men shall I have?
SHAL. Four of which you please.
BARD. Sir, a word with you. I have three pound to free Mouldy and
 Bullcalf.
FAL. Go to; well.
SHAL. Come, Sir John, which four will you have?   240
FAL. Do you choose for me.
SHAL. Marry, then—Mouldy, Bullcalf, Feeble, and Shadow.
FAL. Mouldy and Bullcalf: for you, Mouldy, stay at home till you
 are past service; and for your part, Bullcalf, grow till you come
 unto it. I will none of you.
SHAL. Sir John, Sir John, do not yourself wrong. They are your
 likeliest men, and I would have you serv'd with the best.   249
FAL. Will you tell me, Master Shallow, how to choose a man? Care
 I for the limb, the thews, the stature, bulk, and big assemblance
 of a man! Give me the spirit, Master Shallow. Here's Wart;
 you see what a ragged appearance it is. 'A shall charge you and
 discharge you with the motion of a pewterer's hammer, come off   'come off . . . bucket'
 and on swifter than he that gibbets on the brewer's bucket. And   omitted.
 this same half-fac'd fellow, Shadow—give me this man. He
 presents no mark to the enemy; the foeman may with as great
 aim level at the edge of a penknife. And, for a retreat—how
 swiftly will this Feeble, the woman's tailor, run off! O, give me

the spare men, and spare me the great ones. Put me a caliver
into Wart's hand, Bardolph.   263
BARD. Hold, Wart. Traverse—thus, thus, thus.
FAL. Come, manage me your caliver. So—very well. Go to ; very
good ; exceeding good. O, give me always a little, lean, old,
chopt, bald shot. Well said, i' faith, Wart ; th'art a good scab.
Hold, there's a tester for thee.   269
SHAL. He is not his craft's master, he doth not do it right. I remember
at Mile-end Green, when I lay at Clement's Inn—I was then Sir
Dagonet in Arthur's show—there was a little quiver fellow, and 'a
would manage you his piece thus ; and 'a would about and about,
and come you in and come you in. ' Rah, tah, tah ! ' would 'a
say ; ' Bounce ! ' would 'a say ; and away again would 'a go, and
again would 'a come. I shall ne'er see such a fellow.   278
FAL. These fellows will do well. Master Shallow, God keep you !
Master Silence, I will not use many words with you : Fare you
well ! Gentlemen both, I thank you I must a dozen mile
to-night. Bardolph, give the soldiers coats.   283
SHAL. Sir John, the Lord bless you ; God prosper your affairs ;
God send us peace ! At your return, visit our house ; let our old
acquaintance be renewed. Peradventure I will with ye to the
court.
FAL. Fore God, would you would.
SHAL. Go to ; I have spoke at a word. God keep you.   290
FAL. Fare you well, gentle gentlemen. [*Exeunt* Justices.] On,
Bardolph ; lead the men away. [*Exeunt all but* FALSTAFF.] As I
return, I will fetch off these justices. I do see the bottom of
Justice Shallow. Lord, Lord, how subject we old men are to this
vice of lying ! This same starv'd justice hath done nothing but
prate to me of the wildness of his youth and the feats he hath done
about Turnbull Street ; and every third word a lie, duer paid to
the hearer than the Turk's tribute. I do remember him at
Clement's Inn, like a man made after supper of a cheese-paring.
When 'a was naked, he was for all the world like a fork'd radish,
with a head fantastically carved upon it with a knife. 'A was so
forlorn that his dimensions to any thick sight were invisible. 'A
was the very genius of famine ; yet lecherous as a monkey, and
the whores call'd him mandrake. 'A came ever in the rearward of
the fashion, and sung those tunes to the overscutch'd huswifes
that he heard the carmen whistle, and sware they were his fancies
or his good-nights. And now is this Vice's dagger become a
squire, and talks as familiarly of John a Gaunt as if he had been
sworn brother to him ; and I'll be sworn 'a ne'er saw him but
once in the Tiltyard ; and then he burst his head for crowding
among the marshal's men. I saw it, and told John a Gaunt he
beat his own name ; for you might have thrust him and all his
apparel into an eel-skin ; the case of a treble hautboy was a
mansion for him, a court—and now has he land and beeves.
Well, I'll be acquainted with him if I return ; and 't shall go hard
but I'll make him a philosopher's two stones to me. If the young
dace be a bait for the old pike, I see no reason in the law of nature
but I may snap at him. Let time shape, and there an end. [*Exit.*

For 'give the soldiers
coats' read 'lead the
men away'.

'On, Bardolph ; lead
the men away'
omitted.

'duer paid . . .
tribute' omitted.

''A was so . . .
invisible' omitted.

''A came ever . . .
good-nights' omitted.

'I saw it . . . a court'
omitted.

'and't shall go . . . to
me' omitted.

ACT FOUR.

SCENE I.   *Yorkshire.   Within the Forest of Gaultree.*

Enter the ARCHBISHOP OF YORK, MOWBRAY, HASTINGS, *and* Others.

ARCH. What is this forest call'd ?
HAST. 'Tis Gaultree Forest, an't shall please your Grace.
ARCH. Here stand, my lords, and send discoverers forth
    To know the numbers of our enemies.
HAST. We have sent forth already.
ARCH.   'Tis well done.   5
    My friends and brethren in these great affairs,
    I must acquaint you that I have receiv'd
    New-dated letters from Northumberland ;
    Their cold intent, tenour, and substance, thus :
    Here doth he wish his person, with such powers   10
    As might hold sortance with his quality,
    The which he could not levy ;   whereupon
    He is retir'd, to ripe his growing fortunes,
    To Scotland ; and concludes in hearty prayers
    That your attempts may overlive the hazard   15
    And fearful meeting of their opposite.
MOWB. Thus do the hopes we have in him touch ground
    And dash themselves to pieces.

Enter a Messenger.

HAST.   Now, what news ?
MESS. West of this forest, scarcely off a mile,
    In goodly form comes on the enemy ;   20
    And, by the ground they hide, I judge their number
    Upon or near the rate of thirty thousand.
MOWB. The just proportion that we gave them out.
    Let us sway on and face them in the field.

Enter WESTMORELAND.

ARCH. What well-appointed leader fronts us here ?   25
MOWB. I think it is my Lord of Westmoreland.
WEST. Health and fair greeting from our general,
    The Prince, Lord John and Duke of Lancaster.
ARCH. Say on, my Lord of Westmoreland, in peace,
    What doth concern your coming.
WEST.   Then, my lord,   30
    Unto your Grace do I in chief address
    The substance of my speech.   If that rebellion
    Came like itself, in base and abject routs,
    Led on by bloody youth, guarded with rags,
    And countenanc'd by boys and beggary—   35
    I say, if damn'd commotion so appear'd
    In his true, native, and most proper shape,
    You, reverend father, and these noble lords,
    Had not been here to dress the ugly form
    Of base and bloody insurrection   40
    With your fair honours.   You, Lord Archbishop,

Lines 1-5 omitted.

Lines 25-26 omitted.

Lines 32-41, 'If that
rebellion . . . fair
honours', omitted.

Whose see is by a civil peace maintain'd,
Whose beard the silver hand of peace hath touch'd,
Whose learning and good letters peace hath tutor'd,
Whose white investments figure innocence,   45
The dove, and very blessed spirit of peace—
Wherefore you do so ill translate yourself
Out of the speech of peace, that bears such grace,
Into the harsh and boist'rous tongue of war;
Turning your books to graves, your ink to blood,   50
Your pens to lances, and your tongue divine
To a loud trumpet and a point of war?
ARCH. Wherefore do I this? So the question stands.
Briefly to this end: we are all diseas'd
And with our surfeiting and wanton hours   55
Have brought ourselves into a burning fever,
And we must bleed for it; of which disease
Our late King, Richard, being infected, died.
But, my most noble Lord of Westmoreland,
I take not on me here as a physician;   60
Nor do I as an enemy to peace
Troop in the throngs of military men;
But rather show awhile like fearful war
To diet rank minds sick of happiness,
And purge th' obstructions which begin to stop   65
Our very veins of life. Hear me more plainly.
I have in equal balance justly weigh'd
What wrongs our arms may do, what wrongs we suffer,
And find our griefs heavier than our offences.
We see which way the stream of time doth run   70
And are enforc'd from our most quiet there
By the rough torrent of occasion;
And have the summary of all our griefs,
When time shall serve, to show in articles;
Which long ere this we offer'd to the King,   75
And might by no suit gain our audience:
When we are wrong'd, and would unfold our griefs,
We are denied access unto his person,
Even by those men that most have done us wrong.
The dangers of the days but newly gone,   80
Whose memory is written on the earth
With yet appearing blood, and the examples
Of every minute's instance, present now,
Hath put us in these ill-beseeming arms;
Not to break peace, or any branch of it,   85
But to establish here a peace indeed,
Concurring both in name and quality.
WEST. When ever yet was your appeal denied;
Wherein have you been galled by the King;
What peer hath been suborn'd to grate on you   90
That you should seal this lawless bloody book
Of forg'd rebellion with a seal divine,
And consecrate commotion's bitter edge?
ARCH. My brother general, the commonwealth,
To brother born an household cruelty,   95

Lines 42–46 omitted.

Lines 59–66 omitted.

Lines 80–87 omitted.

Line 95 omitted.

I make my quarrel in particular.
WEST. There is no need of any such redress ;
    Or if there were, it not belongs to you.
MOWB. Why not to him in part, and to us all
    That feel the bruises of the days before,   100
    And suffer the condition of these times
    To lay a heavy and unequal hand
    Upon our honours ?
WEST.   O my good Lord Mowbray,
    Construe the times to their necessities,
    And you shall say, indeed, it is the time,   105
    And not the King, that doth you injuries.
    Yet, for your part, it not appears to me,   Lines 107–139
    Either from the King or in the present time,   omitted.
    That you should have an inch of any ground
    To build a grief on.   Were you not restor'd   110
    To all the Duke of Norfolk's signiories,
    Your noble and right well-rememb'red father's ?
MOWB. What thing, in honour, had my father lost
    That need to be reviv'd and breath'd in me ?
    The King that lov'd him, as the state stood then,   115
    Was force perforce compell'd to banish him,
    And then that Henry Bolingbroke and he,
    Being mounted and both roused in their seats,
    Their neighing coursers daring of the spur,
    Their armed staves in charge, their beavers down,   120
    Their eyes of fire sparkling through sights of steel,
    And the loud trumpet blowing them together—
    Then, then, when there was nothing could have stay'd
    My father from the breast of Bolingbroke,
    O, when the King did throw his warder down—   125
    His own life hung upon the staff he threw—
    Then threw he down himself, and all their lives
    That by indictment and by dint of sword
    Have since miscarried under Bolingbroke.
WEST. You speak, Lord Mowbray, now you know not what.   130
    The Earl of Hereford was reputed then
    In England the most valiant gentleman.
    Who knows on whom fortune would then have smil'd ?
    But if your father had been victor there,
    He ne'er had borne it out of Coventry ;   135
    For all the country, in a general voice,
    Cried hate upon him ; and all their prayers and love
    Were set on Hereford, whom they doted on,
    And bless'd and grac'd indeed more than the King.
    But this is mere digression from my purpose.   140
    Here come I from our princely general
    To know your griefs ; to tell you from his Grace
    That he will give you audience ; and wherein
    It shall appear that your demands are just,
    You shall enjoy them, everything set off   145
    That might so much as think you enemies.
MOWB. But he hath forc'd us to compel this offer ;   Lines 147–167
    And it proceeds from policy, not love.   omitted.

WEST. Mowbray, you overween to take it so.
    This offer comes from mercy, not from fear ;   150
    For, lo ! within a ken our army lies—
    Upon mine honour, all too confident
    To give admittance to a thought of fear.
    Our battle is more full of names than yours,
    Our men more perfect in the use of arms,   155
    Our armour all as strong, our cause the best ;
    Then reason will our hearts should be as good.
    Say you not, then, our offer is compell'd.
MOWB. Well, by my will we shall admit no parley.
WEST. That argues but the shame of your offence :   160
    A rotten case abides no handling.
HAST. Hath the Prince John a full commission,
    In very ample virtue of his father,
    To hear and absolutely to determine
    Of what conditions we shall stand upon ?   165
WEST. That is intended in the general's name.
    I muse you make so slight a question.
ARCH. Then take, my Lord of Westmoreland, this schedule,
    For this contains our general grievances.
    Each several article herein redress'd,   170
    All members of our cause, both here and hence,
    That are insinewed to this action,
    Acquitted by a true substantial form,
    And present execution of our wills
    To us and to our purposes confin'd—   175
    We come within our lawful banks again,
    And knit our powers to the arm of peace.
WEST. This will I show the general.   Please you, lords,
    In sight of both our battles we may meet ;
    And either end in peace—which God so frame !—   180
    Or to the place of diff'rence call the swords
    Which must decide it.
ARCH.   My lord, we will do so.
                [*Exit* WESTMORELAND.
MOWB. There is a thing within my bosom tells me
    That no conditions of our peace can stand.
HAST. Fear you not that : if we can make our peace   185
    Upon such large terms and so absolute
    As our conditions shall consist upon,
    Our peace shall stand as firm as rocky mountains.
MOWB. Yea, but our valuation shall be such
    That every slight and false-derived cause,   190
    Yea, every idle, nice, and wanton reason,
    Shall to the King taste of this action ;
    That, were our royal faiths martyrs in love,
    We shall be winnow'd with so rough a wind
    That even our corn shall seem as light as chaff,   195
    And good from bad find no partition.
ARCH. No, no, my lord.   Note this : the King is weary
    Of dainty and such picking grievances ;
    For he hath found to end one doubt by death
    Revives two greater in the heirs of life ;   200

Lines 147–167
omitted.

Lines 170–177
omitted.

And therefore will he wipe his tables clean,
And keep no tell-tale to his memory
That may repeat and history his loss
To new remembrance. For full well he knows
He cannot so precisely weed this land   205
As his misdoubts present occasion:
His foes are so enrooted with his friends
That, plucking to unfix an enemy,
He doth unfasten so and shake a friend.
So that this land, like an offensive wife   210
That hath enrag'd him on to offer strokes,
As he is striking, holds his infant up,
And hangs resolv'd correction in the arm
That was uprear'd to execution.

HAST. Besides, the King hath wasted all his rods   215
On late offenders, that he now doth lack
The very instruments of chastisement;
So that his power, like to a fangless lion,
May offer, but not hold.

ARCH.   'Tis very true;
And therefore be assur'd, my good Lord Marshal,   220
If we do now make our atonement well,
Our peace will, like a broken limb united,
Grow stronger for the breaking.

MOWB.   Be it so.
Here is return'd my Lord of Westmoreland.

Re-enter WESTMORELAND.

WEST. The Prince is here at hand. Pleaseth your lordship   225
To meet his Grace just distance 'tween our armies?

MOWB. Your Grace of York, in God's name then, set forward.

ARCH. Before, and greet his Grace. My lord, we come. [*Exeunt.*

SCENE II. *Another part of the forest.*

Enter, from one side, MOWBRAY, *attended; afterwards, the* ARCHBISHOP,
HASTINGS, *and* Others: *from the other side,* PRINCE JOHN OF LANCASTER,
WESTMORELAND, Officers *and* Others.

P. JOHN. You are well encount'red here, my cousin Mowbray.
Good day to you, gentle Lord Archbishop;
And so to you, Lord Hastings, and to all.
My Lord of York, it better show'd with you
When that your flock, assembled by the bell,   5
Encircled you to hear with reverence
Your exposition on the holy text
Than now to see you here an iron man,
Cheering a rout of rebels with your drum,
Turning the word to sword, and life to death.   10
That man that sits within a monarch's heart
And ripens in the sunshine of his favour,
Would he abuse the countenance of the king,
Alack, what mischiefs might be set abroach
In shadow of such greatness! With you, Lord Bishop,   15
It is even so. Who hath not heard it spoken

Lines 201–214
omitted.

Lines 227–228
omitted.

In the television
production the action
is continuous, and
there is no scene
change here.

Lines 11–22, '. . .
our dull workings',
omitted.

How deep you were within the books of God ?
To us the speaker in His parliament,
To us th' imagin'd voice of God himself,
The very opener and intelligencer   20
Between the grace, the sanctities of heaven,
And our dull workings. O, who shall believe
But you misuse the reverence of your place,
Employ the countenance and grace of heav'n
As a false favourite doth his prince's name,   25
In deeds dishonourable ? You have ta'en up,
Under the counterfeited zeal of God,
The subjects of His substitute, my father,
And both against the peace of heaven and him
Have here up-swarm'd them.
ARCH.   Good my Lord of Lancaster,   30
I am not here against your father's peace ;
But, as I told my Lord of Westmoreland,
The time misord'red doth, in common sense,
Crowd us and crush us to this monstrous form
To hold our safety up. I sent your Grace   35
The parcels and particulars of our grief,
The which hath been with scorn shov'd from the court,
Whereon this hydra son of war is born ;
Whose dangerous eyes may well be charm'd asleep
With grant of our most just and right desires ;   40
And true obedience, of this madness cur'd,
Stoop tamely to the foot of majesty.
MOWB. If not, we ready are to try our fortunes
To the last man.
HAST.   And though we here fall down,
We have supplies to second our attempt.   45
If they miscarry, theirs shall second them ;
And so success of mischief shall be born,
And heir from heir shall hold this quarrel up
Whiles England shall have generation.
P. JOHN. You are too shallow, Hastings, much too shallow,   50
To sound the bottom of the after-times.
WEST. Pleaseth your Grace to answer them directly
How far forth you do like their articles.
P. JOHN. I like them all and do allow them well ;
And swear here, by the honour of my blood,   55
My father's purposes have been mistook ;
And some about him have too lavishly
Wrested his meaning and authority.
My lord, these griefs shall be with speed redress'd ;
Upon my soul, they shall. If this may please you,   60
Discharge your powers unto their several counties,
As we will ours ; and here, between the armies,
Let's drink together friendly and embrace,
That all their eyes may bear those tokens home
Of our restored love and amity.   65
ARCH. I take your princely word for these redresses.
P. JOHN. I give it you, and will maintain my word ;
And thereupon I drink unto your Grace.

Lines 11–22, '. . .
our dull workings',
omitted.

Lines 41–51 omitted.

HAST. Go, Captain, and deliver to the army
    This news of peace. Let them have pay, and part.   70
    I know it will well please them. Hie thee, Captain.
                   [*Exit* Officer.
ARCH. To you, my noble Lord of Westmoreland.
WEST. I pledge your Grace ; and if you knew what pains
    I have bestow'd to breed this present peace,
    You would drink freely ; but my love to ye   75
    Shall show itself more openly hereafter.
ARCH. I do not doubt you.
WEST.   I am glad of it.
    Health to my lord and gentle cousin, Mowbray.
MOWB. You wish me health in very happy season,
    For I am on the sudden something ill.   80
ARCH. Against ill chances men are ever merry ;
    But heaviness foreruns the good event.
WEST. Therefore be merry, coz ; since sudden sorrow
    Serves to say thus, ' Some good thing comes to-morrow '.
ARCH. Believe me, I am passing light in spirit.   85
MOWB. So much the worse, if your own rule be true.   [*Shouts within.*
P. JOHN. The word of peace is rend'red. Hark, how they shout !
MOWB. This had been cheerful after victory.
ARCH. A peace is of the nature of a conquest ;
    For then both parties nobly are subdu'd,   90
    And neither party loser.
P. JOHN.   Go, my lord,
    And let our army be discharged too.   [*Exit* WESTMORELAND.
    And, good my lord, so please you let our trains
    March by us, that we may peruse the men
    We should have cop'd withal.
ARCH.   Go, good Lord Hastings,   95
    And, ere they be dismiss'd, let them march by.   [*Exit* HASTINGS.
P. JOHN. I trust, lords, we shall lie to-night together.

            Re-enter WESTMORELAND.

    Now, cousin, wherefore stands our army still ?
WEST. The leaders, having charge from you to stand,
    Will not go off until they hear you speak.   100
P. JOHN. They know their duties.

            Re-enter HASTINGS.

HAST. My lord, our army is dispers'd already.
    Like youthful steers unyok'd, they take their courses
    East, west, north, south ; or like a school broke up,
    Each hurries toward his home and sporting-place.   105
WEST. Good tidings, my Lord Hastings ; for the which
    I do arrest thee, traitor, of high treason ;
    And you, Lord Archbishop, and you, Lord Mowbray,
    Of capital treason I attach you both.
MOWB. Is this proceeding just and honourable ?   110
WEST. Is your assembly so ?
ARCH. Will you thus break your faith ?
P. JOHN.   I pawn'd thee none :
    I promis'd you redress of these same grievances

Whereof you did complain ; which, by mine honour,
I will perform with a most Christian care.   115
But for you, rebels—look to taste the due
Meet for rebellion and such acts as yours.
Most shallowly did you these arms commence,
Fondly brought here, and foolishly sent hence.
Strike up our drums, pursue the scatt'red stray.   120
God, and not we, hath safely fought to-day.
Some guard these traitors to the block of death,
Treason's true bed and yielder-up of breath.   [*Exeunt.*]

Lines 122–123
omitted.

SCENE III.   *Another part of the forest.*

Alarum ; excursions.   Enter FALSTAFF *and* COLVILLE, *meeting.*

FAL. What's your name, sir ?   Of what condition are you, and of
what place, I pray ?
COL. I am a knight sir ; and my name is Colville of the Dale.
FAL. Well then, Colville is your name, a knight is your degree, and
your place the Dale.   Colville shall still be your name, a traitor
your degree, and the dungeon your place—a place deep enough ;
so shall you be still Colville of the Dale.
COL. Are not you Sir John Falstaff ?   10
FAL. As good a man as he, sir, whoe'er I am.   Do you yield, sir, or
shall I sweat for you ?   If I do sweat, they are the drops of thy
lovers, and they weep for thy death ; therefore rouse up fear and
trembling, and do observance to my mercy.
COL. I think you are Sir John Falstaff, and in that thought yield me.
FAL. I have a whole school of tongues in this belly of mine ; and not
a tongue of them all speaks any other word but my name.   An I had
but a belly of any indifferency, I were simply the most active
fellow in Europe.   My womb, my womb, my womb undoes me.
Here comes our general.   23

Enter PRINCE JOHN OF LANCASTER, WESTMORELAND, BLUNT, *and* Others.

P. JOHN. The heat is past ; follow no further now.
Call in the powers, good cousin Westmoreland.
                                    [*Exit* WESTMORELAND.
Now, Falstaff, where have you been all this while ?
When everything is ended, then you come.
These tardy tricks of yours will, on my life,
One time or other break some gallows' back.   29
FAL. I would be sorry, my lord, but it should be thus : I never knew
yet but rebuke and check was the reward of valour.   Do you
think me a swallow, an arrow, or a bullet ?   Have I, in my poor and
old motion, the expedition of thought ?   I have speeded hither
with the very extremist inch of possibility ; I have found'red nine
score and odd posts ; and here, travel-tainted as I am, have, in my
pure and immaculate valour, taken Sir John Colville of the Dale,
a most furious knight and valorous enemy.   But what of that ?
He saw me, and yielded ; that I may justly say with the hook-nos'd
fellow of Rome—I came, saw, and overcame.   41
P. JOHN. It was more of his courtesy than your deserving.
FAL. I know not.   Here he is, and here I yield him ; and I beseech
your Grace, let it be book'd with the rest of this day's deeds ; or,

SCENE 13
*Exterior. Another part
of Gaultree Forest.
Day.*
FALSTAFF *and the* BOY
prepare a trap for
COLVILLE.

'If I do
sweat . . . my
mercy' omitted.

'I have a . . . undoes
me' omitted.

'I have found'red . . .
posts' omitted.

by the Lord, I will have it in a particular ballad else, with mine
own picture on the top on't, Colville kissing my foot ; to the
which course if I be enforc'd, if you do not all show like gilt
twopences to me, and I, in the clear sky of fame, o'ershine you
as much as the full moon doth the cinders of the element, which
show like pins' heads to her, believe not the word of the noble.
Therefore let me have right, and let desert mount.   54

'to the which course
. . . of the noble'
omitted.

P. JOHN. Thine's too heavy to mount.
FAL. Let it shine, then.
P. JOHN. Thine's too thick to shine.
FAL. Let it do something, my good lord, that may do me good, and
call it what you will.
P. JOHN. Is thy name Colville ?   60
COL. It is, my lord.
P. JOHN. A famous rebel art thou, Colville.
FAL. And a famous true subject took him.
COL. I am, my lord, but as my betters are
    That led me hither. Had they been rul'd by me,   65
    You should have won them dearer than you have.
FAL. I know not how they sold themselves ; but thou, like a kind
fellow, gavest thyself away gratis ; and I thank thee for thee.

            Re-enter WESTMORELAND.

Omitted.

P. JOHN. Now, have you left pursuit ?   70
WEST. Retreat is made, and execution stay'd.

Lines 70–71 omitted.

P. JOHN. Send Colville, with his confederates,
    To York, to present execution.
    Blunt, lead him hence ; and see you guard him sure.
                [*Exeunt* BLUNT *and* Others.

Line 74 and s.d.
omitted.

    And now dispatch we toward the court, my lords.   75
    I hear the King my father is sore sick.
    Our news shall go before us to his Majesty,
    Which, cousin, you shall bear to comfort him ;
    And we with sober speed will follow you.   79
FAL. My lord, I beseech you, give me leave to go through Gloucestershire ; and, when you come to court, stand my good lord, pray,
in your good report.
P. JOHN. Fare you well, Falstaff. I, in my condition,
    Shall better speak of you than you deserve.   84
                [*Exeunt all but* FALSTAFF.
FAL. I would you had but the wit ; 'twere better than your dukedom.
Good faith, this same young sober-blooded boy doth not love me ;
nor a man cannot make him laugh—but that's no marvel ; he
drinks no wine. There's never none of these demure boys come
to any proof ; for thin drink doth so over-cool their blood, and
making many fish-meals, that they fall into a kind of male green-
sickness ; and then, when they marry, they get wenches. They are
generally fools and cowards—which some of us should be too,
but for inflammation. A good sherris-sack hath a twofold
operation in it. It ascends me into the brain ; dries me there all
the foolish and dull and crudy vapours which environ it ; makes
it apprehensive, quick, forgetive, full of nimble, fiery, and
delectable shapes ; which delivered o'er to the voice, the tongue,
which is the birth, becomes excellent wit. The second property

of your excellent sherris is the warming of the blood; which
before, cold and settled, left the liver white and pale, which is the
badge of pusillanimity and cowardice; but the sherris warms it,
and makes it course from the inwards to the parts extremes. It
illumineth the face, which, as a beacon, gives warning to all the
rest of this little kingdom, man, to arm; and then the vital
commoners and inland petty spirits muster me all to their captain,
the heart, who, great and puff'd up with this retinue, doth any deed
of courage—and this valour comes of sherris. So that skill in
the weapon is nothing without sack, for that sets it a-work; and
learning, a mere hoard of gold kept by a devil till sack commences
it and sets it in act and use. Hereof comes it that Prince Harry
is valiant; for the cold blood he did naturally inherit of his father,
he hath, like lean, sterile, and bare land, manured, husbanded,
and till'd, with excellent endeavour of drinking good and good
store of fertile sherris, that he is become very hot and valiant.
If I had a thousand sons, the first humane principle I would
teach them should be to forswear thin potations, and to addict
themselves to sack.   122

Enter BARDOLPH.

| How now, Bardolph! | Line 123 omitted.
BARD. The army is discharged all and gone.
FAL. Let them go. I'll through Gloucestershire, and there will I
visit Master Robert Shallow, Esquire. I have him already
temp'ring between my finger and my thumb, and shortly will I
seal with him. Come away.   [*Exeunt.*

SCENE IV. *Westminster. The Jerusalem Chamber.*

Enter the KING, PRINCE THOMAS OF CLARENCE, PRINCE HUMPHREY OF
GLOUCESTER, WARWICK, *and* Others.

KING. Now, lords, if God doth give successful end
    To this debate that bleedeth at our doors,
    We will our youth lead on to higher fields,
    And draw no swords but what are sanctified.
    Our navy is address'd, our power collected,   5
    Our substitutes in absence well invested,
    And everything lies level to our wish.
    Only we want a little personal strength;
    And pause us till these rebels, now afoot,
    Come underneath the yoke of government.   10
WAR. Both which we doubt not but your Majesty
    Shall soon enjoy.
KING.   Humphrey, my son of Gloucester,
    Where is the Prince your brother?
P. HUMPH. I think he's gone to hunt, my lord, at Windsor.
KING. And how accompanied?
P. HUMPH.   I do not know, my lord.   15
KING. Is not his brother, Thomas of Clarence, with him?
P. HUMPH. No, my good lord, he is in presence here.
CLA. What would my lord and father?
KING. Nothing but well to thee, Thomas of Clarence.
    How chance thou art not with the Prince thy brother?   20

SCENE 14
*Interior. The Palace of
Westminster. The
Jerusalem Chamber.
Day.*

He loves thee, and thou dost neglect him, Thomas.
Thou hast a better place in his affection
Than all thy brothers ; cherish it, my boy,
And noble offices thou mayst effect
Of mediation, after I am dead,   25
Between his greatness and thy other brethren.
Therefore omit him not ; blunt not his love,
Nor lose the good advantage of his grace
By seeming cold or careless of his will ;
For he is gracious if he be observ'd.   30
He hath a tear for pity and a hand
Open as day for melting charity ;
Yet notwithstanding, being incens'd, he is flint ;
As humorous as winter, and as sudden
As flaws congealed in the spring of day.   35
His temper, therefore, must be well observ'd.
Chide him for faults, and do it reverently,
When you perceive his blood inclin'd to mirth ;
But, being moody, give him line and scope
Till that his passions, like a whale on ground,   40
Confound themselves with working. Learn this, Thomas,
And thou shalt prove a shelter to thy friends,
A hoop of gold to bind thy brothers in,
That the united vessel of their blood,
Mingled with venom of suggestion—   45
As, force perforce, the age will pour it in—
Shall never leak, though it do work as strong
As aconitum or rash gunpowder.
CLA. I shall observe him with all care and love.
KING. Why art thou not at Windsor with him, Thomas ?   50
CLA. He is not there to-day ; he dines in London.
KING. And how accompanied ?   Canst thou tell that ?
CLA. With Poins, and other his continual followers.
KING. Most subject is the fattest soil to weeds ;
And he, the noble image of my youth,
Is overspread with them ; therefore my grief   55
Stretches itself beyond the hour of death.
The blood weeps from my heart when I do shape,
In forms imaginary, th' unguided days
And rotten times that you shall look upon   60
When I am sleeping with my ancestors.
For when his headstrong riot hath no curb,
When rage and hot blood are his counsellors,
When means and lavish manners meet together,
O, with what wings shall his affections fly   65
Towards fronting peril and oppos'd decay !
WOR. My gracious lord, you look beyond him quite.
The Prince but studies his companions
Like a strange tongue, wherein, to gain the language,
'Tis needful that the most immodest word   70
Be look'd upon and learnt ; which once attain'd,
Your Highness knows, comes to no further use
But to be known and hated.   So, like gross terms,
The Prince will, in the perfectness of time,

Cast off his followers ; and their memory   75
  Shall as a pattern or a measure live
  By which his Grace must mete the lives of other,
  Turning past evils to advantages.
KING. 'Tis seldom when the bee doth leave her comb
  In the dead carrion.

Enter WESTMORELAND.

           Who's here ? Westmoreland ?   80
WEST. Health to my sovereign, and new happiness
  Added to that that I am to deliver !
  Prince John, your son, doth kiss your Grace's hand.
  Mowbray, the Bishop Scroop, Hastings, and all,
  Are brought to the correction of your law.   85
  There is not now a rebel's sword unsheath'd,
  But Peace puts forth her olive everywhere.
  The manner how this action hath been borne | Lines 88–90 omitted.
  Here at more leisure may your Highness read,
  With every course in his particular.   90
KING. O Westmoreland, thou art a summer bird,
  Which ever in the haunch of winter sings
  The lifting up of day.

Enter HARCOURT.   Omitted.

        Look, here's more news.   Lines 93–96 omitted.
HAR. From enemies heaven keep your Majesty ;   WEST. And here's
  And, when they stand against you, may they fall   95   more news.
  As those that I am come to tell you of !   Lines 97–99 are
  The Earl Northumberland and the Lord Bardolph,   spoken by
  With a great power of English and of Scots,   WESTMORELAND.
  Are by the shrieve of Yorkshire overthrown.   Lines 100–101
  The manner and true order of the fight   100   omitted.
  This packet, please it you, contains at large.
KING. And wherefore should these good news make me sick ?
  Will Fortune never come with both hands full,
  But write her fair words still in foulest letters ?
  She either gives a stomach and no food—   105
  Such are the poor, in health—or else a feast,
  And takes away the stomach—such are the rich
  That have abundance and enjoy it not.
  I should rejoice now at this happy news ;
  And now my sight fails, and my brain is giddy.   110
  O me ! come near me now I am much ill.
P. HUMPH. Comfort, your Majesty !
CLA.   O my royal father !
WEST. My sovereign lord, cheer up yourself, look up.
WAR. Be patient, Princes ; you do know these fits
  Are with his Highness very ordinary.   115
  Stand from him, give him air ; he'll straight be well.   The KING is borne
CLA. No, no ; he cannot long hold out these pangs.   into the adjoining
  Th' incessant care and labour of his mind   room.
  Hath wrought the mure that should confine it in
  So thin that life looks through, and will break out. 120
P. HUMPH. The people fear me ; for they do observe | Lines 121–129
                        omitted.

Unfather'd heirs and loathly births of nature.
The seasons change their manners, as the year
Had found some months asleep, and leapt them over.
CLA. The river hath thrice flow'd, no ebb between ;   125
And the old folk, Time's doting chronicles,
Say it did so a little time before
That our great grandsire, Edward, sick'd and died.
WAR. Speak lower, Princes, for the King recovers.
P. HUMPH. This apoplexy will certain be his end.   130
KING. I pray you take me up, and bear me hence
Into some other chamber. Softly, pray.

SCENE V.   *Westminster.   Another chamber.*

The KING *lying on a bed ;* CLARENCE, GLOUCESTER, WARWICK, *and*
Others *in attendance.*

KING. Let there be no noise made, my gentle friends ;
Unless some dull and favourable hand
Will whisper music to my weary spirit.
WAR. Call for the music in the other room.
KING. Set me the crown upon my pillow here.   5
CLA. His eye is hollow, and he changes much.
WAR. Less noise, less noise !

Enter PRINCE HENRY.

PRINCE. Who saw the Duke of Clarence ?
CLA. I am here, brother, full of heaviness.
PRINCE. How now !   Rain within doors, and none abroad !
How doth the King ?   10
P. HUMPH. Exceeding ill.
PRINCE.   Heard he the good news yet ? Tell it him.
P. HUMPH. He alt'red much upon the hearing it.
PRINCE. If he be sick with joy, he'll recover without physic.   15
WAR. Not so much noise, my lords.   Sweet Prince, speak low ;
The King your father is dispos'd to sleep.
CLA. Let us withdraw into the other room.
WAR. Will't please your Grace to go along with us ?
PRINCE. No ; I will sit and watch here by the King.   20
                    [*Exeunt all but the* Prince.
Why doth the crown lie there upon his pillow,
Being so troublesome a bedfellow ?
O polish'd perturbation ! golden care !
That keep'st the ports of slumber open wide
To many a watchful night !   Sleep with it now !   25
Yet not so sound and half so deeply sweet
As he whose brow with homely biggen bound
Snores out the watch of night.   O majesty !
When thou dost pinch thy bearer, thou dost sit
Like a rich armour worn in heat of day   30
That scald'st with safety.   By his gates of breath
There lies a downy feather which stirs not.
Did he suspire, that light and weightless down
Perforce must move.   My gracious lord ! my father !
This sleep is sound indeed ; this is a sleep   35

Lines 121–129
omitted.

SCENE 15
*Interior. The King's
Bedroom adjoining the
Jerusalem Chamber.
Day.*
The KING is helped to
his bed.
'I pray you . . .
chamber' omitted.

Lines 1–7 omitted.

SCENE 16
*Interior. The
Jerusalem Chamber.
Day.*

Spoken by CLARENCE

Spoken by CLARENCE
After line 14, PRINCE
HENRY, followed by
CLARENCE, goes into
the adjoining room.
At line 15:
SCENE 17
*Interior. The King's
Bedroom. Day.*
The KING, WARWICK,
Lords. PRINCE
HENRY joins them.

Line 18 spoken by
WARWICK.

That from this golden rigol hath divorc'd
So many English kings. Thy due from me
Is tears and heavy sorrows of the blood
Which nature, love, and filial tenderness,
Shall, O dear father, pay thee plenteously.   40
My due from thee is this imperial crown,
Which, as immediate from thy place and blood,
Derives itself to me. [*Putting on the crown.*]   Lo where it sits—
Which God shall guard ; and put the world's whole strength
Into one giant arm, it shall not force   45
This lineal honour from me. This from thee
Will I to mine leave as 'tis left to me.   [*Exit.*
KING. Warwick ! Gloucester ! Clarence !

Re-enter WARWICK, GLOUCESTER, CLARENCE.

CLA. Doth the King call ?
WAR. What would your Majesty ? How fares your Grace ?   50
KING. Why did you leave me here alone, my lords ?
CLA. We left the Prince my brother here, my liege,
     Who undertook to sit and watch by you.
KING. The Prince of Wales ! Where is he ? Let me see him.
     He is not here.   55
WAR. This door is open ; he is gone this way.
P. HUMPH. He came not through the chamber where we stay'd.
KING. Where is the crown ? Who took it from my pillow ?
WAR. When we withdrew, my liege, we left it here.
KING. The Prince hath ta'en it hence. Go, seek him out.   60
     Is he so hasty that he doth suppose
     My sleep my death ?
     Find him, my Lord of Warwick ; chide him hither. [*Exit* WARWICK.
     This part of his conjoins with my disease
     And helps to end me. See, sons, what things you are ! 65
     How quickly nature falls into revolt
     When gold becomes her object !
     For this the foolish over-careful fathers
     Have broke their sleep with thoughts,
     Their brains with care, their bones with industry; 70
     For this they have engrossed and pil'd up
     The cank'red heaps of strange-achieved gold ;
     For this they have been thoughtful to invest
     Their sons with arts and martial exercises ;
     When, like the bee, tolling from every flower   75
     The virtuous sweets,
     Our thighs with wax, our mouths with honey pack'd,
     We bring it to the hive, and, like the bees,
     Are murd'red for our pains. This bitter taste
     Yields his engrossments to the ending father.   80

Re-enter WARWICK.

     Now where is he that will not stay so long
     Till his friend sickness hath determin'd me ?
WAR. My lord, I found the Prince in the next room,
     Washing with kindly tears his gentle cheeks,
     With such a deep demeanour in great sorrow,   85

| Lines 71–72 omitted.

| Lines 80–88 omitted.

Prince Hal (David Gwillim) with the King (Jon Finch)

That tyranny, which never quaff'd but blood,
Would, by beholding him, have wash'd his knife
With gentle eye-drops.   He is coming hither.
KING. But wherefore did he take away the crown ?

Re-enter PRINCE HENRY.

Lo where he comes.   Come hither to me, Harry.   90
Depart the chamber, leave us here alone.
          [*Exeunt all but the* KING *and the* PRINCE.
PRINCE. I never thought to hear you speak again.
KING. Thy wish was father, Harry, to that thought.
I stay too long by thee, I weary thee.
Dost thou so hunger for mine empty chair   95
That thou wilt needs invest thee with my honours
Before thy hour be ripe ?   O foolish youth !
Thou seek'st the greatness that will overwhelm thee.
Stay but a little, for my cloud of dignity
Is held from falling with so weak a wind   100
That it will quickly drop ; my day is dim.
Thou hast stol'n that which, after some few hours,
Were thine without offence ; and at my death
Thou hast seal'd up my expectation.
Thy life did manifest thou lov'dst me not,   105
And thou wilt have me die assur'd of it.
Thou hid'st a thousand daggers in thy thoughts,
Which thou hast whetted on thy stony heart,
To stab at half an hour of my life.
What, canst thou not forbear me half an hour ?   110
Then get thee gone, and dig my grave thyself ;
And bid the merry bells ring to thine ear
That thou art crowned, not that I am dead.
Let all the tears that should bedew my hearse
Be drops of balm to sanctify thy head ;   115
Only compound me with forgotten dust ;
Give that which gave thee life unto the worms.
Pluck down my officers, break my decrees ;
For now a time is come to mock at form—
Harry the Fifth is crown'd.   Up, vanity :   120
Down, royal state.   All you sage counsellors, hence.
And to the English court assemble now,
From every region, apes of idleness.
Now, neighbour confines, purge you of your scum.
Have you a ruffian that will swear, drink, dance,   125
Revel the night, rob, murder, and commit
The oldest sins the newest kind of ways ?
Be happy, he will trouble you no more.
England shall double gild his treble guilt ;
England shall give him office, honour, might ;   130
For the fifth Harry from curb'd license plucks
The muzzle of restraint, and the wild dog
Shall flesh his tooth on every innocent.
O my poor kingdom, sick with civil blows !
When that my care could not withhold thy riots,   135
What wilt thou do when riot is thy care ?

Lines 80–88 omitted.

Lines 107–109
omitted

Lines 124–130
omitted.

O, thou wilt be a wilderness again.
Peopled with wolves, thy old inhabitants !
PRINCE. O, pardon me, my liege !   But for my tears,
    The moist impediments unto my speech,   140
    I had forestall'd this dear and deep rebuke
    Ere you with grief had spoke and I had heard
    The course of it so far.   There is your crown,
    And he that wears the crown immortally
    Long guard it yours ! [*Kneeling*.]   If I affect it more   145
    Than as your honour and as your renown,
    Let me no more from this obedience rise,
    Which my most inward true and duteous spirit
    Teacheth this prostrate and exterior bending !
    God witness with me, when I here came in   150
    And found no course of breath within your Majesty,
    How cold it struck my heart !   If I do feign,
    O, let me in my present wildness die,
    And never live to show th' incredulous world
    The noble change that I have purposed !   155
    Coming to look on you, thinking you dead—
    And dead almost, my liege, to think you were—
    I spake unto this crown as having sense,
    And thus upbraided it :   ' The care on thee depending
    Hath fed upon the body of my father ;   160
    Therefore thou best of gold art worst of gold.
    Other, less fine in carat, is more precious,
    Preserving life in med'cine potable ;
    But thou, most fine, most honour'd, most renown'd,
    Hast eat thy bearer up '.   Thus, my most royal liege,   165
    Accusing it, I put it on my head,
    To try with it—as with an enemy
    That had before my face murd'red my father—
    The quarrel of a true inheritor.
    But if it did infect my blood with joy,   170
    Or swell my thoughts to any strain of pride ;
    If any rebel or vain spirit of mine
    Did with the least affection of a welcome
    Give entertainment to the might of it,
    Let God for ever keep it from my head,   175
    And make me as the poorest vassal is,
    That doth with awe and terror kneel to it !
KING.   O my son,
    God put it in thy mind to take it hence,
    That thou mightst win the more thy father's love,   180
    Pleading so wisely in excuse of it !
    Come hither, Harry ; sit thou by my bed,
    And hear, I think, the very latest counsel
    That ever I shall breathe.   God knows, my son,
    By what by-paths and indirect crook'd ways   185
    I met this crown ; and I myself know well
    How troublesome it sat upon my head :
    To thee it shall descend with better quiet,
    Better opinion, better confirmation ;
    For all the soil of the achievement goes   190

With me into the earth.   It seem'd in me
But as an honour snatch'd with boist'rous hand ;
And I had many living to upbraid
My gain of it by their assistances ;
Which daily grew to quarrel and to bloodshed,   195
Wounding supposed peace.   All these bold fears
Thou seest with peril I have answered ;
For all my reign hath been but as a scene
Acting that argument.   And now my death
Changes the mood ; for what in me was purchas'd   200
Falls upon thee in a more fairer sort ;
So thou the garland wear'st successively.
Yet, though thou stand'st more sure than I could do,
Thou art not firm enough, since griefs are green ;
And all my friends, which thou must make thy friends,   205
Have but their stings and teeth newly ta'en out ;
By whose fell working I was first advanc'd,
And by whose power I well might lodge a fear
To be again displac'd ; which to avoid,
I cut them off ; and had a purpose now   210
To lead out many to the Holy Land,
Lest rest and lying still might make them look
Too near unto my state.   Therefore, my Harry,
Be it thy course to busy giddy minds
With foreign quarrels, that action, hence borne out,   215
May waste the memory of the former days.   The KING is here in
More would I, but my lungs are wasted so   some distress, and
That strength of speech is utterly denied me.   WARWICK and others
How I came by the crown, O God, forgive ;   return in alarm to the
And grant it may with thee in true peace live !   220 King's presence.
PRINCE. My gracious liege,
    You won it, wore it, kept it, gave it me ;
    Then plain and right must my possession be ;
    Which I with more than with a common pain
    'Gainst all the world will rightfully maintain.   225

Enter PRINCE JOHN OF LANCASTER, WARWICK, LORDS, *and* Others.	Omitted.
KING. Look, look, here comes my John of Lancaster.	Lines 226–232
P. JOHN. Health, peace, and happiness, to my royal father !	omitted.

KING. Thou bring'st me happiness and peace, son John ;
    But health, alack, with youthful wings is flown
    From this bare wither'd trunk.   Upon thy sight   230
    My worldly business makes a period.
    Where is my Lord of Warwick ?
PRINCE.   My Lord of Warwick !
KING. Doth any name particular belong
    Unto the lodging where I first did swoon ?
WAR. 'Tis call'd Jerusalem, my noble lord.   235
KING. Laud be to God !   Even there my life must end.
    It hath been prophesied to me many years,
    I should not die but in Jerusalem ;
    Which vainly I suppos'd the Holy Land.
    But bear me to that chamber ; there I'll lie ;   240
    In that Jerusalem shall Harry die.   [*Exeunt.*

ACT FIVE.

SCENE I. *Gloucestershire.   Shallow's house.*

Enter SHALLOW, FALSTAFF, BARDOLPH, *and* Page.

SHAL. By cock and pie, sir, you shall not away to-night.   What, Davy, I say!

FAL. You must excuse me, Master Robert Shallow.

SHAL. I will not excuse you ; you shall not be excus'd ; excuses shall not be admitted ; there is no excuse shall serve ; you shall not be excus'd.   Why, Davy!   6

Enter DAVY.

DAVY. Here, sir.

SHAL. Davy, Davy, Davy, Davy ; let me see, Davy ; let me see, Davy ; let me see—yea, marry, William cook, bid him come hither.   Sir John, you shall not be excus'd.

DAVY. Marry, sir, thus : those precepts cannot be served ; and, again, sir—shall we sow the headland with wheat ?

SHAL. With red wheat, Davy.   But for William cook—are there no young pigeons ?   16

DAVY. Yes, sir.   Here is now the smith's note for shoeing and plough-irons.

SHAL. Let it be cast, and paid.   Sir John, you shall not be excused.

DAVY. Now, sir, a new link to the bucket must needs be had ; and, sir, do you mean to stop any of William's wages about the sack he lost the other day at Hinckley fair ?   24

SHAL. 'A shall answer it.   Some pigeons, Davy, a couple of short-legg'd hens, a joint of mutton, and any pretty little tiny kickshaws, tell William cook.

DAVY. Doth the man of war stay all night, sir ?

SHAL. Yea, Davy ; I will use him well.   A friend i' th' court is better than a penny in purse.   Use his men well, Davy ; for they are arrant knaves and will backbite.

DAVY. No worse than they are backbitten, sir ; for they have marvellous foul linen.   34

SHAL. Well conceited, Davy—about thy business, Davy.

DAVY. I beseech you, sir, to countenance William Visor of Woncot against Clement Perkes o' th' hill.

SHAL. There is many complaints, Davy, against that Visor.   That Visor is an arrant knave, on my knowledge.   39

DAVY. I grant your worship that he is a knave, sir ; but yet God forbid, sir, but a knave should have some countenance at his friend's request.   An honest man, sir, is able to speak for himself, when a knave is not.   I have serv'd your worship truly, sir, this eight years ; an I cannot once or twice in a quarter bear out a knave against an honest man, I have but a very little credit with your worship.   The knave is mine honest friend, sir ; therefore, I beseech you, let him be countenanc'd.   49

SHAL. Go to ;   I say he shall have no wrong.   Look about, Davy. [*Exit* DAVY.]   Where are you, Sir John ?   Come, come, come, off with your boots.   Give me your hand, Master Bardolph.

BARD. I am glad to see your worship.

SCENE 18
*Exterior.
Gloucestershire.
Outside Shallow's
House. Night.*

'I beseech you . . .
[*Exit* DAVY]' omitted.

SHAL. I thank thee with all my heart, kind Master Bardolph. [*To the*
     Page.] And welcome, my tall fellow. Come, Sir John.   57
FAL. I'll follow you, good master Robert Shallow. [*Exit* SHALLOW.]
     Bardolph, look to our horses. [*Exeunt* BARDOLPH *and* Page.] If I
     were sawed into quantities, I should make four dozen of such
     bearded hermits' staves as Master Shallow. It is a wonderful
     thing to see the semblable coherence of his men's spirits and his.
     They, by observing of him, do bear themselves like foolish justices:
     he, by conversing with them, is turned into a justice-like serving-
     man. Their spirits are so married in conjunction with the
     participation of society that they flock together in consent, like
     so many wild geese. If I had a suit to Master Shallow, I would
     humour his men with the imputation of being near their master;
     if to his men, I would curry with Master Shallow that no man
     could better command his servants. It is certain that either wise
     bearing or ignorant carriage is caught, as men take diseases, one
     of another; therefore let men take heed of their company. I will
     devise matter enough out of this Shallow to keep Prince Harry
     in continual laughter the wearing out of six fashions, which is four
     terms, or two actions; and 'a shall laugh without intervallums.
     O, it is much that a lie with a slight oath, and a jest with a sad brow
     will do with a fellow that never had the ache in his shoulders!
     O, you shall see him laugh till his face be like a wet cloak ill laid up!
SHAL. [*Within.*] Sir John!   83
FAL. I come, Master Shallow; I come, Master Shallow.   [*Exit.*

             SCENE II. *Westminster. The palace.*

     Enter, severally, WARWICK, *and the* LORD CHIEF JUSTICE.

WAR. How now, my Lord Chief Justice; whither away?
CH. JUST. How doth the King?
WAR. Exceeding well; his cares are now all ended.
CH. JUST. I hope, not dead.
WAR.   He's walk'd the way of nature;
     And to our purposes he lives no more.   5
CH. JUST. I would his Majesty had call'd me with him.
     The service that I truly did his life
     Hath left me open to all injuries.
WAR. Indeed, I think the young king loves you not.
CH. JUST. I know he doth not, and do arm myself   10
     To welcome the condition of the time,
     Which cannot look more hideously upon me
     Than I have drawn it in my fantasy.

Enter LANCASTER, CLARENCE, GLOUCESTER, WESTMORELAND, *and* Others.

WAR. Here comes the heavy issue of dead Harry.
     O that the living Harry had the temper   15
     Of he, the worst of these three gentlemen!
     How many nobles then should hold their places
     That must strike sail to spirits of vile sort!
CH. JUST. O God, I fear all will be overturn'd.
P. JOHN. Good morrow, cousin Warwick, good morrow.   20
GLOU. ⎫
CLAR. ⎬ Good morrow, cousin.

SHALLOW shepherds
them all into the
house.
At line 57:
SCENE 19
Interior.
Gloucestershire. A
Room in Shallow's
House. Night.

'Their spirits . . . his
servants' omitted.

'the wearing out . . .
his shoulders!'
omitted.

SHALLOW calls from
the next room.

SCENE 20
Interior. The Palace of
Westminster. The
Jerusalem Chamber.
Day.

Line 1 omitted.

Lines 20–42 omitted.

P. JOHN. We meet like men that had forgot to speak.

WAR. We do remember; but our argument
    Is all too heavy to admit much talk.

P. JOHN. Well, peace be with him that hath made us heavy!   25

CH. JUST. Peace be with us, lest we be heavier!

P. HUMPH. O, good my lord, you have lost a friend indeed;
    And I dare swear you borrow not that face
    Of seeming sorrow—it is sure your own.

P. JOHN. Though no man be assur'd what grace to find,   30
    You stand in coldest expectation.
    I am the sorrier; would 'twere otherwise.

CLA. Well, you must now speak Sir John Falstaff fair;
    Which swims against your stream of quality.

CH. JUST. Sweet Princes, what I did, I did in honour,   35
    Led by th' impartial conduct of my soul;
    And never shall you see that I will beg
    A ragged and forestall'd remission.
    If truth and upright innocency fail me,
    I'll to the King my master that is dead,   40
    And tell him who hath sent me after him.

WAR. Here comes the Prince.

        Enter KING HENRY THE FIFTH, *attended.*

CH. JUST. Good morrow, and God save your Majesty!

KING. This new and gorgeous garment, majesty,
    Sits not so easy on me as you think.   45
    Brothers, you mix your sadness with some fear.
    This is the English, not the Turkish court;
    Not Amurath an Amurath succeeds,
    But Harry Harry. Yet be sad, good brothers,
    For, by my faith, it very well becomes you.   50
    Sorrow so royally in you appears
    That I will deeply put the fashion on,
    And wear it in my heart. Why, then, be sad;
    But entertain no more of it, good brothers,
    Than a joint burden laid upon us all.   55
    For me, by heaven, I bid you be assur'd,
    I'll be your father and your brother too;
    Let me but bear your love, I'll bear your cares.
    Yet weep that Harry's dead, and so will I;
    But Harry lives that shall convert those tears   60
    By number into hours of happiness.

BROTHERS. We hope no otherwise from your Majesty.

KING. You all look strangely on me; and you most.
    You are, I think, assur'd I love you not.

CH. JUST. I am assur'd, if I be measur'd rightly,   65
    Your Majesty hath no just cause to hate me.

KING. No?
    How might a prince of my great hopes forget
    So great indignities you laid upon me?
    What, rate, rebuke, and roughly send to prison,   70
    Th' immediate heir of England! Was this easy?
    May this be wash'd in Lethe and forgotten?

CH. JUST. I did then use the person of your father;

Lines 20–42 omitted.

Spoken by P. JOHN
only.

The image of his power lay then in me ;
And in th' administration of his law,   75
Whiles I was busy for the commonwealth,
Your Highness pleased to forget my place,
The majesty and power of law and justice,
The image of the King whom I presented,
And struck me in my very seat of judgment ;   80
Whereon, as an offender to your father,
I gave bold way to my authority
And did commit you. If the deed were ill,
Be you contented, wearing now the garland,
To have a son set your decrees at nought,   85
To pluck down justice from your awful bench,
To trip the course of law, and blunt the sword
That guards the peace and safety of your person ;
Nay, more, to spurn at your most royal image, | Lines 89–94 omitted.
And mock your workings in a second body.   90
Question your royal thoughts, make the case yours ;
Be now the father, and propose a son ;
Hear your own dignity so much profan'd,
See your most dreadful laws so loosely slighted,
Behold yourself so by a son disdain'd ;   95
And then imagine me taking your part
And, in your power, soft silencing your son.
After this cold considerance, sentence me ;
And, as you are king, speak in your state
What I have done that misbecame my place,   100
My person, or my liege's sovereignty.
KING. You are right, Justice, and you weigh this well ;
Therefore still bear the balance and the sword ;
And I do wish your honours may increase
Till you do live to see a son of mine   105
Offend you, and obey you, as I did.
So shall I live to speak my father's words :
' Happy am I that have a man so bold
That dares do justice on my proper son ;
And not less happy, having such a son   110
That would deliver up his greatness so
Into the hands of justice '. You did commit me ;
For which I do commit into your hand
Th' unstained sword that you have us'd to bear ;
With this remembrance—that you use the same   115
With the like bold, just, and impartial spirit
As you have done 'gainst me. There is my hand.
You shall be as a father to my youth ;
My voice shall sound as you do prompt mine ear ;
And I will stoop and humble my intents   120
To your well-practis'd wise directions.
And, Princes all, believe me, I beseech you,
My father has gone wild into his grave,
For in his tomb lie my affections ;
And with his spirits sadly I survive,   125
To mock the expectation of the world,
To frustrate prophecies, and to raze out

Rotten opinion, who hath writ me down
After my seeming.   The tide of blood in me
Hath proudly flow'd in vanity till now.   130
Now doth it turn and ebb back to the sea,
Where it shall mingle with the state of floods,
And flow henceforth in formal majesty.
Now call we our high court of parliament ;
And let us choose such limbs of noble counsel,   135
That the great body of our state may go
In equal rank with the best govern'd nation ;
That war, or peace, or both at once, may be
As things acquainted and familiar to us ;
In which you, father, shall have foremost hand.   140
Our coronation done, we will accite,
As I before rememb'red, all our state ;
And—God consigning to my good intents—
No prince nor peer shall have just cause to say,
God shorten Harry's happy life one day.   [*Exeunt.*   All say: God save the
                                                               King.

SCENE III.   *Gloucestershire.   Shallow's orchard.*   SCENE 21

Enter FALSTAFF, SHALLOW, SILENCE, BARDOLPH, *the* Page, *and* DAVY.   *Exterior.*
                                                               Gloucestershire.
SHAL. Nay, you shall see my orchard, where, in an arbour, we will   *Outside Shallow's*
    eat a last year's pippin of mine own graffing, with a dish of   *House. Day.*
    caraways, and so forth.   Come, cousin Silence.   And then to bed.
FAL. Fore God, you have here a goodly dwelling and rich.
SHAL. Barren, barren, barren ; beggars all, beggars all, Sir John—
    marry, good air.   Spread, Davy, spread, Davy ; well said, Davy.
FAL. This Davy serves you for good uses ; he is your serving-man
    and your husband.   11
SHAL. A good varlet, a good varlet, a very good varlet, Sir John.
    By the mass, I have drunk too much sack at supper.   A good
    varlet.   Now sit down, now sit down ; come, cousin.
SIL. Ah, sirrah ! quoth-a—we shall   [*Singing.*
        Do nothing but eat and make good cheer,
        And praise God for the merry year ;
        When flesh is cheap and females dear,
        And lusty lads roam here and there,   20
            So merrily,
        And ever among so merrily.
FAL. There's a merry heart !   Good Master Silence, I'll give you a
    health for that anon.
SHAL. Give Master Bardolph some wine, Davy.   25
DAVY. Sweet sir, sit ; I'll be with you anon ; most sweet sir, sit. | 'Proface' omitted.
    Master Page, good Master Page, sit.   Proface !   What you want
    in meat, we'll have in drink.   But you must bear ; the heart's all.
                                                      [*Exit.*
SHAL. Be merry, Master Bardolph ; and, my little soldier there, be
    merry.   31
SIL. [*Singing.*]
        Be merry, be merry, my wife has all ;
        For women are shrews, both short and tall ;
        'Tis merry in hall when beards wag all ;

And welcome merry Shrove-tide.   35
Be merry, be merry.

FAL. I did not think Master Silence had been a man of this mettle.
SIL. Who, I ? I have been merry twice and once ere now.

Re-enter DAVY.

DAVY. [*To* BARDOLPH.] There's a dish of leather-coats for you.
SHAL. Davy!
DAVY. Your worship! I'll be with you straight. [*To* BARDOLPH.] A
cup of wine, sir ?
SIL. [*Singing*]
A cup of wine that's brisk and fine,
And drink unto the leman mine ;
And a merry heart lives long-a.
FAL. Well said, Master Silence.
SIL. An we shall be merry, now comes in the sweet o' th' night.   50
FAL. Health and long life to you, Master Silence !
SIL. [*Singing.*]
Fill the cup, and let it come,
I'll pledge you a mile to th' bottom.
SHAL. Honest Bardolph, welcome ; if thou want'st anything and wilt
not call, beshrew thy heart. Welcome, my little tiny thief and
welcome indeed too. I'll drink to Master Bardolph, and to all
the cabileros about London.   58
DAVY. I hope to see London once ere I die.
BARD. An I might see you there, Davy !   60
SHAL. By the mass, you'll crack a quart together—ha ! will you not,
Master Bardolph ?
BARD. Yea, sir, in a pottle-pot.
SHAL. By God's liggens, I thank thee. The knave will stick by thee,
I can assure thee that. 'A will not out, 'a ; 'tis true bred.   66
BARD. And I'll stick by him, sir.
SHAL. Why, there spoke a king. Lack nothing ; be merry. [*One
knocks at door.*] Look who's at door there, ho ! Who knocks ?
                                                    [*Exit* DAVY.
FAL. [*To* SILENCE, *who has drunk a bumper.*] Why, now you have done
me right.
SIL. [*Singing.*]
Do me right,
And dub me knight.
Samingo.
Is't not so ?   75
FAL. 'Tis so.
SIL. Is't so ? Why then, say an old man can do somewhat.

Re-enter DAVY.

DAVY. An't please your worship, there's one Pistol come from the
court with news.   80
FAL. From the court ? Let him come in.

Enter PISTOL.

How now, Pistol ?
PIST. Sir John, God save you !
FAL. What wind blew you hither, Pistol ?

'Be merry, be merry'
omitted.
Lines 38–77, 'Who, I
. . . do somewhat',
omitted.

Gordon Gostelow as Bardolph and Anthony Quayle as Falstaff

PIST. Not the ill wind which blows no man to good.   Sweet knight,
    thou art now one of the greatest men in this realm.
SIL. By'r lady, I think 'a be, but goodman Puff of Barson.
PIST. Puff!   90
    Puff in thy teeth, most recreant coward base!
    Sir John, I am thy Pistol and thy friend,
    And helter-skelter have I rode to thee;
    And tidings do I bring, and lucky joys,
    And golden times, and happy news of price.   95
FAL. I pray thee now, deliver them like a man of this world.
PIST. A foutra for the world and worldlings base!
    I speak of Africa and golden joys.
FAL. O base Assyrian knight, what is thy news?   100
    Let King Cophetua know the truth thereof.
SIL. [Singing.] And Robin Hood, Scarlet, and John.
PIST. Shall dunghill curs confront the Helicons?
    And shall good news be baffled?
    Then, Pistol, lay thy head in Furies' lap.   105
SHAL. Honest gentleman, I know not your breeding.
PIST. Why, then, lament therefore.
SHAL. Give me pardon, sir.   If, sir, you come with news from the
    court, I take it there's but two ways—either to utter them or
    conceal them.   I am, sir, under the King, in some authority.
PIST. Under which king, Bezonian?   Speak, or die.
SHAL. Under King Harry.
PIST.   Harry the Fourth—or Fifth?
SHAL. Harry the Fourth.
PIST.   A foutra for thine office!
    Sir John, thy tender lambkin now is King;   115
    Harry the Fifth's the man.   I speak the truth.
    When Pistol lies, do this; and fig me, like
    The bragging Spaniard.
FAL. What, is the old king dead?
PIST. As nail in door.   The things I speak are just.   120
FAL. Away, Bardolph! saddle my horse.   Master Robert Shallow,
    choose what office thou wilt in the land, 'tis thine.   Pistol, I will
    double-charge thee with dignities.
BARD. O joyful day!   125
    I would not take a knighthood for my fortune.
PIST. What, I do bring good news?
FAL. Carry Master Silence to bed.   Master Shallow, my Lord
    Shallow, be what thou wilt—I am Fortune's steward.   Get on
    thy boots;   we'll ride all night.   O sweet Pistol!   Away,
    Bardolph! [Exit BARDOLPH.] Come, Pistol, utter more to me;
    and withal devise something to do thyself good.   Boot, boot,
    Master Shallow!   I know the young King is sick for me.   Let us
    take any man's horses: the laws of England are at my command-
    ment.   Blessed are they that have been my friends;   and woe to
    my Lord Chief Justice!   137
PIST. Let vultures vile seize on his lungs also!
    'Where is the life that late I led?' say they.
    Why, here it is; welcome these pleasant days!   [Exeunt.

Side notes (right margin):

'By'r lady . . . coward base' omitted.

Lines 102–107 omitted.

'Carry Master Silence to bed' omitted.

'Come, Pistol . . . thyself good' omitted.

Lines 138–140 omitted.

SCENE IV. *London. A street.*

Enter BEADLES, *dragging in* HOSTESS QUICKLY *and* DOLL TEARSHEET.

HOST. No, thou arrant knave ; I would to God that I might die, that I might have thee hang'd. Thou hast drawn my shoulder out of joint.

1 BEAD. The constables have delivered her over to me ; and she shall have whipping-cheer enough, I warrant her. There hath been a man or two lately kill'd about her.

DOLL. Nut-hook, nut-hook, you lie. Come on ; I'll tell thee what, thou damn'd tripe-visag'd rascal, an the child I now go with do miscarry, thou wert better thou hadst struck thy mother, thou paper-fac'd villain.							11

HOST. O the Lord, that Sir John were come ! He would make this a bloody day to somebody. But I pray God the fruit of her womb miscarry !

1 BEAD. If it do, you shall have a dozen of cushions again ; you have but eleven now. Come, I charge you both go with me ; for the man is dead that you and Pistol beat amongst you.				18

DOLL. I'll tell you what, you thin man in a censer, I will have you as soundly swing'd for this—you blue-bottle rogue, you filthy famish'd correctioner, if you be not swing'd, I'll forswear half-kirtles.

1 BEAD. Come, come, you she knight-errant, come.

HOST. O God, that right should thus overcome might ! Well, of sufferance comes ease.							25

DOLL. Come, you rogue, come ; bring me to a justice.

HOST. Ay, come, you starv'd bloodhound.

DOLL. Goodman death, goodman bones !

HOST. Thou atomy, thou !

DOLL. Come, you thin thing ! come, you rascal !			30

1 BEAD. Very well.					[*Exeunt.*

SCENE V. *Westminster. Near the Abbey.*

Enter Grooms, *strewing rushes.*

1 GROOM. More rushes, more rushes !

2 GROOM. The trumpets have sounded twice.

3 GROOM. 'Twill be two o'clock ere they come from the coronation. Dispatch, dispatch.					[*Exeunt.*

Trumpets sound, and the KING *and his* Train *pass over the stage. After them enter* FALSTAFF, SHALLOW, PISTOL, BARDOLPH, *and* Page.

FAL. Stand here by me, Master Robert Shallow ; I will make the King do you grace. I will leer upon him, as 'a comes by ; and do but mark the countenance that he will give me.

PIST. God bless thy lungs, good knight !				9

FAL. Come here, Pistol ; stand behind me. [*To* SHALLOW.] O, if I had had time to have made new liveries, I would have bestowed the thousand pound I borrowed of you. But 'tis no matter ; this poor show doth better ; this doth infer the zeal I had to see him.										14

SHAL. It doth so.

This scene omitted.

SCENE 22
Exterior. London. A Street. Day.
FALSTAFF, SHALLOW,
PISTOL, BARDOLPH,
Page & Citizens.

Lines 1–4 and s.d. omitted.

FAL. It shows my earnestness of affection—
SHAL. It doth so.
FAL. My devotion—
SHAL. It doth, it doth, it doth.
FAL. As it were, to ride day and night ; and not to deliberate, not to
    remember, not to have patience to shift me—   22
SHAL. It is best, certain.
FAL. But to stand stained with travel, and sweating with desire to
    see him ; thinking of nothing else, putting all affairs else in
    oblivion, as if there were nothing else to be done but to see him.
PIST. 'Tis ' semper idem ' for ' obsque hoc nihil est '. 'Tis all in | Lines 28–40 omitted.
    every part.   29
SHAL. 'Tis so, indeed.
PIST. My knight, I will inflame thy noble liver
    And make thee rage.
    Thy Doll, and Helen of thy noble thoughts,
    Is in base durance and contagious prison ;
    Hal'd thither   35
    By most mechanical and dirty hand.
    Rouse up revenge from ebon den with fell Alecto's snake,
    For Doll is in. Pistol speaks nought but truth.
FAL. I will deliver her.   [*Shouts within, and the trumpets sound.*
PIST. There roar'd the sea, and trumpet-clangor sounds.   40

Enter the KING *and his* Train, *the* LORD CHIEF JUSTICE *among them.*

FAL. God save thy Grace, King Hal ; my royal Hal !
PIST. The heavens thee guard and keep, most royal imp of fame !
FAL. God save thee, my sweet boy !
KING. My Lord Chief Justice, speak to that vain man.   45
CH. JUST. Have you your wits ? Know you what 'tis you speak ?
FAL. My king ! my Jove ! I speak to thee, my heart !
KING. I know thee not, old man. Fall to thy prayers.
    How ill white hairs become a fool and jester !
    I have long dreamt of such a kind of man,   50
    So surfeit-swell'd, so old, and so profane ;
    But being awak'd, I do despise my dream.
    Make less thy body hence, and more thy grace ;
    Leave gormandizing ; know the grave doth gape
    For thee thrice wider than for other men—   55
    Reply not to me with a fool-born jest ;
    Presume not that I am the thing I was,
    For God doth know, so shall the world perceive,
    That I have turn'd away my former self ;
    So will I those that kept me company.   60
    When thou dost hear I am as I have been,
    Approach me, and thou shalt be as thou wast,
    The tutor and the feeder of my riots.
    Till then I banish thee, on pain of death,
    As I have done the rest of my misleaders,   65
    Not to come near our person by ten mile.
    For competence of life I will allow you,
    That lack of means enforce you not to evils
    And, as we hear you do reform yourselves,
    We will, according to your strengths and qualities,   70

Give you advancement. Be it your charge, my lord,
To see perform'd the tenour of our word.
Set on.   [*Exeunt the* KING *and his train.*
FAL. Master Shallow, I owe you a thousand pounds.
SHAL. Yea, marry, Sir John; which I beseech you to let me have
  home with me.   76
FAL. That can hardly be, Master Shallow. Do not you grieve at
  this; I shall be sent for in private to him. Look you, he must
  seem thus to the world. Fear not your advancements; I will be
  the man yet that shall make you great.   81
SHAL. I cannot perceive how, unless you give me your doublet, and
  stuff me out with straw. I beseech you, good Sir John, let me
  have five hundred of my thousand.
FAL. Sir, I will be as good as my word. This that you heard was but
  a colour.
SHAL. A colour that I fear you will die in, Sir John.
FAL. Fear no colours; go with me to dinner. Come, Lieutenant
  Pistol; come, Bardolph. I shall be sent for soon at night.   91

  Re-enter PRINCE JOHN, *the* LORD CHIEF JUSTICE, *with* Officers.

CH. JUST. Go, carry Sir John Falstaff to the Fleet;
  Take all his company along with him.
FAL. My lord, my lord—
CH. JUST. I cannot now speak. I will hear you soon.
  Take them away.
PIST. Si fortuna me tormenta, spero me contenta.
            [*Exeunt all but* PRINCE JOHN *and the* LORD CHIEF JUSTICE.
P. JOHN. I like this fair proceeding of the King's.
  He hath intent his wonted followers
  Shall all be very well provided for;   100
  But all are banish'd till their conversations
  Appear more wise and modest to the world.
CH. JUST. And so they are.
P. JOHN. The King hath call'd his parliament, my lord.
CH. JUST. He hath.   105
P. JOHN. I will lay odds that, ere this year expire,
  We bear our civil swords and native fire
  As far as France. I heard a bird so sing,
  Whose music, to my thinking, pleas'd the King.
  Come, will you hence?   [*Exeunt.* | Line 110 omitted.

EPILOGUE.

First my fear, then my curtsy, last my speech. My fear, is your | Epilogue omitted.
displeasure; my curtsy, my duty; and my speech, to beg your
pardons. If you look for a good speech now, you undo me; for
what I have to say is of mine own making; and what, indeed,
I should say will, I doubt, prove mine own marring. But to the
purpose, and so to the venture. Be it known to you, as it is very
well, I was lately here in the end of a displeasing play, to pray
your patience for it and to promise you a better. I meant,
indeed, to pay you with this; which if like an ill venture it come
unluckily home, I break, and you, my gentle creditors, lose.
Here I promis'd you I would be, and here I commit my body to
your mercies. Bate me some, and I will pay you some, and, as

most debtors do, promise you infinitely ; and so I kneel down
before you—but, indeed, to pray for the Queen.   16
If my tongue cannot entreat you to acquit me, will you command me
to use my legs ?   And yet that were but light payment—to dance
out of your debt.   But a good conscience will make any possible
satisfaction, and so would I.   All the gentlewomen here have
forgiven me.   If the gentlemen will not, then the gentlemen do
not agree with the gentlewomen, which was never seen before in
such an assembly.   24
One word more, I beseech you.   If you be not too much cloy'd with
fat meat, our humble author will continue the story, with Sir John
in it, and make you merry with fair Katherine of France ; where,
for anything I know, Falstaff shall die of a sweat, unless already
'a be killed with your hard opinions ; for Oldcastle died a martyr
and this is not the man.   My tongue is weary; when my legs are
too, I will bid you good night.   33

Epilogue omitted.

GLOSSARY

Scott Shane

'"Accommodated"! It comes of accommodo. Very good; a good phrase.'
— Shallow

Difficult phrases are listed under the most important or most difficult word in them. If no such word stands out, they are listed under the first word.

Words appear in the form they take in the text. If they occur in several forms, they are listed under the root form (singular for nouns, infinitive for verbs).

Line references are given only when the same word is used with different meanings, and when there are puns.

Line numbers for prose passages are counted from the last numbered line before the line referred to (since the numbers given do not always correspond to those in this edition).

'A, he
ABATED, (i) blunted (like a sword); (ii) diminished (pun, I i 117)
ABIDE A FIELD, endure a battlefield
ABILITY, ability to pay
ABROACH, 'set abroach', let loose
ABROAD, at large, out of doors
ACCITE, (i) induce, incite (II ii 54); (ii) summon (V i 141)
ACCOMMODATED, provided, equipped (the word was coming into vogue in Shakespeare's time)
ACHE, (i) from bearing great responsibilities; (ii) from being infected with venereal disease (pun, V i 77)
ACHITOPHEL, Biblical counsellor who betrayed David (see 2 Samuel xv, 12ff.)
ACONITUM, a poison
ACTIONS, lawsuits (each of which drags on for two terms)
ADDRESS'D, prepared
ADMITS, associates with
ADVICE, i.e. a doctor's advice
ADVIS'D, aware (I i 172)
AFFECT, desire
AFFECTION, (i) inclination (II iii 29, IV v 173); (ii) appetite, lust (IV iv 65, V ii 124)
AFORE, before
AFRICA, i.e. the source of gold (Pistol speaks

in his ranting manner, imitative of earlier English drama)
AGAINST, before (IV ii 81)
AGAMEMNON, valiant leader of Greek forces against Troy
AGGRAVATE, the Hostess's mistake for 'moderate'
ALARUM, trumpet-call signalling the advance into battle
ALECTO, one of the Furies (who were depicted as having snakes in their hair)
ALEWIFE'S NEW PETTICOAT, i.e. barmaid's red petticoat (associated with prostitutes)
ALLOW, 'allow the occasion of', admit that we have good reason for; 'allow them well', thoroughly approve them
ALTHÆA'S DREAM, that her son would live only as long as a brand burned in the fire (the dream the Page describes was Hecuba's)
AMONGST YOU, between the two of you
AMURATH, Turkish sultan who had all his brothers strangled when he inherited the throne
AN, if
ANATOMIZE, dissect, describe in detail
ANCIENT, ensign (military rank)
ANGEL, 'ill angel', (i) bad angel (as each person was said to have a good and a bad

95

angel) (I ii 154); (ii) clipped angel (a gold coin) (I ii 155)

ANOINTED, i.e. with consecrated oil at his coronation

ANON, soon, in a minute; 'Anon, anon, sir', Francis' repeated call in the joke played on him in *1 Henry IV*, II iv 35ff.

ANSWER, be held responsible for (V i 25)

APOPLEXY, paralysis

APPEARANCE OF THE KING, i.e. noblemen disguised as the King to confuse the enemy

APPERTINENT TO, belonging to

APPLE-JOHN, variety of apple eaten after the skin has wrinkled

APPLIANCES AND MEANS TO BOOT, possible measures taken to bring on sleep, in addition

APPREHENSIVE, quick to perceive

APPROVE, prove

ARGUMENT, subject matter (of a play, IV v 199); for conversation, V ii 23)

ARRANT, out-and-out, absolute

ARTHUR'S SHOW, annual archery display on Mile-End Green in which contestants took the names of King Arthur's knights

ARTICLES, a formal itemised listing (of grievances)

ARTS, liberal arts, learning

ASSEMBLANCE, appearance

ASSURANCE, security (for offering credit)

ASSYRIAN KNIGHT, i.e. heathen robber (Falstaff adopts Pistol's ranting dramatic style)

AT FULL, in full

AT LARGE, in full

ATOMY, the Hostess's mistake for 'anatomy' (skeleton)

ATONEMENT, reconciliation

ATROPOS, the mythological Fate who cut the thread of life

ATTACH, arrest, seize

ATTEND, await

AVAUNT, leave

AVOIRDUPOIS, weight

AWAY WITH, put up with

AWFUL, commanding awe

BACKBITTEN, i.e. by lice

BACKSWORD, stick with a protective hilt used by novice swordsmen

BAFFLED, treated with contempt

BALANCE AND THE SWORD, symbols of the Lord Chief Justice's office

BALM, consecrated oil used in the coronation of a king

BAND, bond

BARBARY HEN, guinea hen; slang for 'prostitute'

BARE-HEADED, i.e. in such haste that they'd left their hats behind

BARTHOLOMEW BOAR-PIG, pig fattened for roasting at London's annual Bartholomew Fair

BASKET-HILT STALE JUGGLER, old-fashioned imposter of a soldier (swords with basket-shaped steel hilts were out of date)

BATE, 'breeds no bate', causes no quarrelling (i.e. Poins tells indiscreet stories); 'Bate me some', release me from some of my debt

BATTLE, (i) line of troops (III ii 152); (ii) army (IV i 154, 179)

BAWDY-HOUSE, brothel

BAWL, 'those that bawl out of the ruins of thy linen', the illegitimate children you have fathered on visits to brothels financed by pawning your linen (or, whose clothes have been made from your linen)

BEADLES, parish officers who punished minor offences

BEAR, (i) know (II ii 15); (ii) be tolerant (V iii 28); (iii) support (a man's weight); (iv) bear children (pun on (ii), (iii) and (iv), II iv 56); 'bear . . . in hand', encourage with false expectations; 'bear out a knave', support a scoundrel

BEARING, conduct

BEAVERS, visors (on their helmets)

BED-HANGERS, bed-curtains (on a four-poster bed)

BEEVES, beef-cattle

BEFITS, 'well befits', is very appropriate

BEFORE, go before us (IV i 228)

BEING, occurrence (I i 179)

BELIE, tell lies about

BELIKE, it is likely

BEROD, bear-herd, a man who looked after tame bears

BESEEK, beseech, beg

BESHREW, shame on

BESTOW, (i) behave (II ii 163); (ii) spend (V v 11)

BESTRIDE, stand over in order to protect (the land, which is like a wounded soldier)

BEST-TEMPER'D, of the finest quality (like the 'temper' of steel)

BEZONIAN, ignorant and impoverished recruit

BIGGEN, nightcap

BIGNESS, 'of a bigness', of equal size (leg size and shape were important for fashionable men)

BILLOWS, waves

BLEED, (i) be bled by a doctor, as a remedy for disease; (ii) shed blood in battle (pun, IV i 57)

BLOCK OF DEATH, executioner's block

BLOOD, mood (II iii 30, IV iv 38, IV v 170)

BLUE-BOTTLE, i.e. wearing a blue uniform (as beadles did)

BLUNT, dull-witted (Ind 18)

BLUSHING, i.e. possessed of a red drinker's complexion

BOIST'ROUS, rough, violent

BOLINGBROKE, Henry IV

BONA-ROBA, high-class prostitute

BOOK'D, noted by the chroniclers travelling with the Prince

BOOK-OATH, oath sworn on a Bible

BOOKS OF GOD, (i) works of divinity; (ii) God's grace (pun, IV ii 17)

BOOT (v.), put on your boots

BORNE, laden (II iv 351); 'borne it out of', carried the prize away from; 'hence borne out', carried on abroad

BORROWER'S CAP, i.e. which is always ready to be removed ingratiatingly to the lender

BOUNCE, i.e. 'bang!'

BOUND, (i) obliged (III ii 166); (ii) covered (IV v 27)

BOW'D, 'necessity so bow'd the state That', the crown's dignity was brought so low that of necessity

BRAVE, defy

BRAWL, 'as the times do brawl', in these tumultuous times

BRAWN, fattened pig

BREACH, gap in military fortification (with sexual suggestion, like most of this speech)

BREAK, (i) break my promise; (ii) go bankrupt (pun, Epil 10)

BREATHE, (i) rest (I i 38); (ii) restore to life and breath (IV i 114); (iii) utter (IV v 184)

BREEDING, parentage, rank

BROADSIDES, volleys from a battery of cannons

BROTHER GENERAL, brothers in the general sense, fellow men

BRUITED, reported

BUCKLER, small shield

BUMPER, tankard filled to the brim

BUNG, pickpocket

BURNS, causes to burn (with venereal disease) (II iv 326)

BURST, broke (III ii 310)

BUSSES, kisses

BY YEA AND NO, mild Puritan oath

CABILEROS, gallants, fine fellows

CAESAR'S FORTUNES, Julius Caesar's military triumphs

CAIN, traditionally the first murderer (see Genesis iv)

CALIPOLIS, character in George Peele's *The Battle of Alcazar* (1594), which this line misquotes

CALIVER, light musket

CALM, the Hostess's mistake for 'qualm'

CANARIES, Canary wine

CANDLE-MINE, i.e. mine of animal fat from which candles could be made

CANKERS (n.), canker-worms (parasites that attacked roses and other plants)

CANK'RED, tarnished

CANOPIES, i.e. bed-canopies

CANVASS, toss (with sexual suggestion)

CAPABLE OF, susceptible to

CAPER, compete in dancing

CARAT, quality

CARAWAYS, caraway seeds or cakes containing them

CARMEN, cart-drivers

CARRIAGE, behaviour

CARRION, decaying flesh

CASE, 'in good case', well-off

CAST, totalled (V i 19); 'cast th'event', estimated the consequences; 'cast him up', vomit him, rebel against him

CATASTROPHE, i.e. rear end

CATCH OF YOU, i.e. catch venereal disease from you (though Doll takes 'catch' to mean 'grab')

CAUSE ON FOOT, dispute with troops marching on both sides

CENSER, 'thin man in a censer', decorative figure of a man stamped on the lid of a perfuming pan

CERBERUS, three-headed dog that guarded the underworld (Pistol makes him a king)

CERTIFICATE, license, legal document (very formal in style)

CHAIR, throne

CHAMBERS, (i) small cannons (with sexual suggestion) (II iv 51); (ii) bedrooms (often 'perfum'd' against mustiness by well-to-do-Elizabethans) (III i 12)

CHANCE, 'is chanced', has occurred; 'How chance it', how does it happen

CHANGES MUCH, turns very pale

CHANNEL, gutter

CHAPS, cheeks

CHARACTERS, (i) letters; (ii) characteristics (pun, I ii 169)

CHARG'D CHAMBERS, loaded cannons (with sexual suggestion)

CHARGE (n.), (i) commission for the command of troops (I ii 58); (ii) position for the charge (IV i 120); (iii) orders (IV ii 99); (iv) responsibility (V v 71); (v.), (i) load a gun (III ii 253); (ii) drink a toast to (puns on (i) and (ii), with sexual suggestion, II iv 105, 114–15); (iii) order (V iv 16)

CHEATER, card-sharper, confidence man

CHECK, rebuke

CHEERING, inciting

CHEESE-PARING, 'made after supper of a cheese-paring', carved in a moment of leisure from a scrap of cheese

CHIEF, 'in chief', in the main

CHIPP'D BREAD, cut the hard crusts off bread

CHOICE, high quality

CHOLER, anger

CHOPS, i.e. fat-cheeks

CHOPT, chapped, dried-up

CHURCH, 'like a church', i.e. not at all

CHURLISH, brutal

CINDERS OF THE ELEMENT, stars of the sky

CIVIL, (i) orderly, well-behaved (II iv 84, 290, IV i 42); (ii) between the citizens of one country (IV v 134, V v 107); 'civil swords', i.e. swords that have recently been used in civil war

CLAPP'D I' TH' CLOUT AT TWELVE SCORE, hit the bull's-eye at 240 yards

CLEAN, altogether (I ii 91)

CLEMENT'S INN, one of the Inns of Chancery (considered inferior to the Inns of Court)

CLOSE (adj.), nearby; (v.), (i) grapple (II i 18); (ii) make peace (II iv 314)

COCK, 'By cock and pie', a mild oath

COFFERS, money-chests

COIF, nightcap

COLDEST, gloomiest

COLOUR, (i) excuse (I ii 231); (ii) pretence (V v 86); (iii) 'choler', anger; (iv) 'collar', hang-man's noose (pun on (ii), (iii) and (iv), V v 87); 'Fear no colours', fear nothing (proverbial)

COMB, 'leave her comb', abandon her honeycomb, even though it is

COMMANDMENT, 'at commandment', for the asking

COMMENCES IT, licenses it to act (as a university student was licensed at 'Commencement')

COMMISSION, 'in commission with me', a justice of the peace, like me

COMMIT, imprison (I ii 50, V ii 83, 112)

COMMODITY, profit

COMMON SENSE, everyone's judgement

COMMONS, common people

COMMONWEALTH, common people (I iii 87)

COMMOTION, rebellion

COMPANION, fellow (a contemptuous term) (II iv 88, 115)

COMPETENCE OF LIFE, means sufficient to live on

COMPLICES, comrades

COMPOUND (n.), lump; (v.), mix

CONCEIT (n.), imagination; (v.), 'Well conceited', very witty

CONCEIVE, 'takes upon him not to conceive', pretends not to understand

CONDITION, (i) rank (IV iii 1); (ii) capacity as military commander (IV iii 83)

CONFINES, 'neighbour confines', nearby regions

CONFIRMATION, legal validity

CONFIRMITIES, the Hostess's mistake for 'infirmities'

CONFOUND, consume

CONGER, eel; 'conger and fennel', eel (supposed to dull the wits) with fennel sauce

CONSENT (n.), unanimity; (v.), agree

CONSIDERANCE, 'cold considerance', cool consideration

CONSIGNING, consenting

CONSIST, insist

CONSTRUE THE TIMES TO THEIR NECESSITIES, understand the present state of affairs as resulting from inevitable forces

CONTAGIOUS, disease-breeding

CONTENTION, strife; 'feed contention in a ling'ring act', maintain strife in a prolonged dispute

CONTINENT, (i) land-mass (III i 47); (ii) contents; (iii) 'continence', chastity (pun on (i), (ii) and (iii), II iv 275)

CONTINUANTLY, the Hostess's mix-up of 'continually' and 'incontinently', immediately
CONVERSATIONS, behaviour
CONVERSING, associating
COOK, 'William cook', William the cook
COP'D WITHAL, fought with
COPHETUA, 'King Cophetua', African king in a contemporary ballad
COPY AND BOOK, pattern and object of study
CORN, grain
CORPORATE, Bullcalf's mistake for 'corporal'
CORPSE, bodies (without souls)
CORRECTIONER, officer of the House of Correction, Bridewell (where prostitutes were punished)
COSTERMONGERS', i.e. materialistic (a costermonger sold apples and other fruit)
COTSOLE, Cotswold (a range of hills in Gloucestershire)
COUNTENANCE, support, favour
COUNTER, 'hunt counter', follow the wrong trail, are mistaken
COURSE, 'every course in his particular', each event described in detail
COURSERS, swift horses
COUSIN, COZ, title of respect (not always indicating a blood relationship)
COVER, lay the tablecloth
CRACK (n.), lively boy; (v), drink
CRAFTY-SICK, pretending to be sick
CRIBS, hovels
CROSSES, (i) hardships (III i 55); (ii) coins stamped with a cross (pun, I ii 213)
CROWN, coin worth five shillings (II ii 87)
CRUDY, curdled, thick
CURRENT, genuine
CURRY WITH, flatter
CURTSY, bow (by a person of either sex); 'make curtsy', bow politely
CUSHIONS, i.e. one of which (the Beadle thinks) Doll is using to feign pregnancy
CUT-PURSE, petty thief, pickpocket
CUTTLE, thieve's knife used for slitting purses; i.e. cut-purse, pickpocket

DACE, small fish used as bait
DAGONET, 'Sir Dagonet', King Arthur's fool
DAINTY, trivial
DALE, valley
DAME, wife
DARING OF THE SPUR, challenging the spur to set them off
DAUGHTER, i.e. daughter-in-law (II iii 1, 46)

DAY, victory (I i 52)
DEAFING, deafening
DEAR, (i) heartfelt (IV v 141); (ii) expensive (V iii 18)
DEATH'S-HEAD, skull or figure of a skull used as a reminder of mortality
DEBATE, conflict
DEBUTY, deputy of the ward, charged with keeping order
DEEPLY, solemnly (V ii 52)
DEGREE, rank (IV iii 4, 6); 'degrees prevent my curses', stages in life have curses which anticipate mine
DEMURE, solemn
DEPENDING, 'care on thee depending', anxiety caused by thee
DERIVE, 'How is this deriv'd?', what's the source of this news?; 'Derives from heaven', claims God's approval for; 'Derives itself', descends
DESCENSION, 'heavy descension', great descent
DESIRE, ask (II i 91, 93)
DETERMIN'D, put an end to
DINT, force
DISCHARGE, (i) fire a gun (III ii 254); (ii) drink a toast to in return (puns on (i) and (ii), with sexual suggestion, II iv 106–7)
DISCOLOURS THE COMPLEXION OF, brings a blush to
DISCOVERERS, scouts
DISPATCH, hurry
DISTEMPERED, 'yet distempered', as yet only sick
DISTRACTED HER, driven her mad
DIVERS, various
DIVINATION LIES, prophecy is false
DOIT, name meaning 'half-farthing'
DOLE, dealing out
DOLL, common name for a prostitute
DOLPHIN CHAMBER, a room in the tavern
DOUBLE-CHARGE, (i) load (a pistol) with a double charge of powder; (ii) heap (with honours) (pun, V iii 123)
DOUBLET, close-fitting jacket
DOUBT (n.), i.e. dangerous enemy (IV i 199); (v.), fear (Epilogue 5)
DOUGLAS, the Earl of Douglas (who kills several noblemen and attacks King Henry in *1 Henry IV*)
DRAM, 'make some dram of a scruple', feel some small doubt (both 'dram' and 'scruple' are small weights used to measure doses of medicine)

DRAW, 'draw our numbers', gather our troops; 'draw the action', withdraw the lawsuit

DRAWER, tavern waiter

DROLLERY, comic picture

DROOPING, i.e. where the sun sets

DROPS OF THY LOVERS, tears of your friends

DUER, more faithfully

DULL, producing drowsiness (IV v 2)

DUMBE, i.e. a preacher who reads out others' sermons rather than composing his own

DURANCE, imprisonment

EASTCHEAP, street and district in London

EASY, insignificant (V ii 71)

EBON, ebony-black

EDGE, (i) narrow path along a ridge (I i 170); (ii) sword (IV i 93)

EDWARD, King Edward III

EFFECT, 'in th'effect of your reputation', in accordance with the reputation you claim

ELDER, (i) old man; (ii) elder tree (pun, II iv 247)

ELM, 'dead elm', noted for rapid rotting

END TRY THE MAN, the man be judged by how he ends up (proverbial)

ENDEAR'D, bound by duty and affection

ENDING, dying (IV v 80)

ENFORCE, force

ENFORCEMENT, 'Upon enforcement', i.e. being pushed or thrown

ENGAGED TO, involved in

ENGRAFFED, attached

ENGROSSED, collected

ENGROSSMENTS, 'This bitter taste Yields his engrossments', his accumulations yield this bitter taste

ENLARGE, add to the significance of

ENTERTAIN NO MORE OF IT, take it as no more

ENTERTAINMENT, reception

ENT'RED THE ACTION, filed the lawsuit

EPHESIANS, good drinking companions (St Paul's Epistle to the Ephesians warns against excess, specifically in wine-drinking)

EQUAL, impartial (IV i 67)

ERE, before

EREBUS, the underworld

ESQUIRE, gentleman ranking just below a knight

ETCETERAS, 'are etceteras nothings?', can we not go further? ('etcetera' and 'nothing' were both euphemisms for the female genitals)

EVEN WAY, smooth passage, assent

EVER AMONG, all the while

EXCURSIONS, sorties, charges into battle

EXION, action, lawsuit

EXPEDITION, rapidity (IV iii 33)

EXTRAORDINARILY, the Hostess's mistake for 'ordinarily', regularly

FACE-ROYAL, (i) a very fine face; (ii) the King's face, stamped on the 'face' of the royal, a ten-shilling coin (pun, I ii 19–20)

FAIN, (i) content (II i 136); (ii) gladly (II iii 65, II iv 11)

FAIRER, 'in a more fairer sort', in a more valid way

FAITORS, impostors

FALL, 'fall foul for toys', quarrel over trifles; 'Fall to', begin

FAMILIARITY, the Hostess's mistake for 'familiar'

FAMILIARS, close friends

FAMOUS, notorious

FANCIES, improvisations

FANTASTICALLY, strangely

FANTASY, imagination

FASHIONS, i.e. fads (which change every couple of months)

FATTEST, most fertile

FAULT, lack (II ii 36); 'in the fault', to be blamed (for their illegitimacy)

FAVOURABLE, kindly

FEAR (n.), danger (I i 95, IV v 196); (v.), (i) frighten (IV iv 121); (ii) doubt (V v 79)

FELL, (i) fierce (IV v 207); (ii) cruel (V v 37)

FETCH OFF, get the better of

FIG ME, LIKE THE BRAGGING SPANIARD, give me the fig (a gesture of contempt), as they do in Spain

FIGURE (n.), design (I iii 43); (v.), (i) reproduce (III i 81); (ii) symbolise (IV i 45)

FILE, roll (listing soldiers)

FILLIP ME WITH A THREE-MAN BEE-TLE, hit me with a sledgehammer so large that it takes three men to wield it

FIND, 'what grace to find', what favour he will receive (from the new King)

FIREBRAND, burning coal

FIST, punch

FIT, sickness

FLAP-DRAGONS, game in which lighted 'candles' ends' were floated on liquor and the player attempted to snatch them out in his mouth or to drink the concoction

FLAWS CONGEALED, icy gusts of wind

FLEDGE, covered with down

FLEET, Fleet prison in London (used for the temporary detention of distinguished prisoners)

FLESH (n.), meat (with sexual suggestion) (II iv 331, V iii 19); (v.), 'flesh'd with conquest', made eager by a taste of victory; 'flesh his tooth on', bite

FLOODS, 'state of floods', majesty of the oceans

FLOW'D, flooded (IV iv 125)

FOEMAN, enemy

FOIN, thrust with a weapon (with sexual suggestion)

FOND MANY, foolish multitude

FONDLY, foolishly

FOOLISH-COMPOUNDED, made up of folly

FOOT, 'under my foot', at my command

FORBEAR, endure

FORCE PERFORCE, of necessity

FORE, before

FOREHAND, 'carried you a forehand shaft a fourteen and fourteen and a half', shot with a straight aim (rather than in a curved trajectory) 280 or 290 yards

FORGETIVE, inventive

FORGOT TO, forgotten how to

FORK'D, i.e. two-legged

FORLORN, scrawny

FORM, 'necessary form of this', inevitable operation of this principle of historical analogy; 'goodly form', well-ordered formation; 'true substantial form', valid and genuine agreement; 'mock at form', ridicule law and order

FORSPENT, worn out

FORSWEAR, swear off, give up; 'forswear keeping house', give up my tavern

FORTIFY IN PAPER, gather our strength only on paper

FORTUNE'S STEWARD, i.e. the man who can distribute Fortune's rewards

FORTY, forty shillings or £2

FORWARD, eager (I i 173)

FOUND'RED, lamed

FOUTRA, obscene expression of contempt; 'a foutra for', i.e. to hell with

FRAME (v.), bring to pass

FRANK, pig-sty (possibly this alludes to the Boar's Head tavern in Eastcheap)

FRENCH CROWNS, coins worth four shillings each (of which he apparently offers five, or £1)

FRIENDS, 'of good friends', from a good family

FRONT, confront

FRUITERER, fruitseller

FUBB'D OFF, put off

FURIES, terrible avenging goddesses of classical mythology

FUSTIAN, ranting, bombastic

FUSTILARIAN, invented word, probably from 'fustilugs', meaning 'a fat, slovenly woman'

GADSHILL, site of robbery committed by Falstaff and his fellows (see *1 Henry IV*, II ii and II iv)

GAINSAID, contradicted

GALEN, second-century Greek physician

GALL (v.), injure, afflict

GALLOWAY NAGS, prostitutes (literally, small Scottish horses)

GALLS (n.), bile (bitter secretion of the liver)

GAMBOL, playful

GAN VAIL HIS STOMACH, began to fail in courage

GARLAND, crown

GATES OF BREATH, mouth and nose

GAULTREE, royal forest in Yorkshire

GAUNTLET, 'scaly gauntlet', armoured glove made of overlapping pieces of metal

GENERATION, offspring

GENIUS, spirit

GENTLE, of noble birth

GERMAN HUNTING, the boar-hunt in Germany (a popular subject for wall-paintings)

GET, beget (II ii 9, IV iii 91)

GIBBETS ON THE BREWER'S BUCKET, hangs buckets of liquor on the carrier's yoke

GIDDY, unstable

GILT TWOPENCES TO ME, counterfeit coins compared to me (silver two-penny pieces were gilded to look like gold half-crowns)

GIRD, mock

GIVE, 'give fire', shoot; 'gave them out', estimated them to be

GLASS, (i) 'glasses is the only drinking', i.e. glasses are now in fashion, so it's not a bad thing to pawn your metal tankards; (ii) mirror (II iii 21, 31)

GLUTTON, Dives, the rich man in Luke xvi, 19–31, who burned in hell (and asked for water to cool his tongue) (I ii 32)

GO, (i) walk; (ii) be accepted as good money (pun, I ii 157); 'Go to', expression of disapproval, impatience or disbelief; 'go with', am pregnant with (V iv 8)

GOOD WILL, 'do my good will', do my best

GOODMAN, title of respect used for men below the rank of gentleman (used ironically, V iv 28)

GOOD-NIGHTS, serenades

GOOD-YEAR, 'What the good-year!', exclamation equivalent to 'What the devil!'

GOSSIP, familiar term of address, equivalent to 'neighbour'

GOT, begotten

GOUT, disease associated with large amounts of rich food and drink

GOWN, dressing-gown (sick man's garment) (III ii 180)

GRACE, (n.), (i) favour (IV ii 24, IV iv 28, V ii 30, V v 6); (ii) royal title (as in 'Your grace') (pun on (i) and (ii), I ii 23); (iii) religious grace, chance of salvation (V v 53); 'right fencing grace', proper form in fencing; (v.), lend credit to (I i 129)

GRAFFING, grafting

GRANDSIRE, grandfather

GRATIS, free of charge

GRAVY, (i) gravy (with pun on 'hair' as 'hare'); (ii) sweat (pun, I ii 153)

GRAY'S INN, one of the Inns of Court

GREEN, fresh, unhealed

GREEN-SICKNESS, a form of anaemia affecting young women

GRIEF, (i) physical pain (I i 144, first use); (ii) sorrow (I i 144, second use); (iii) grievance (IV i 69, 73, 77, 110, 142, IV ii 36, 59, IV v 204)

GROATS, four-penny coins

GROOM, servant

GROSS TERMS, foul language

GROUND, 'ground and vantage', the military advantage; 'on ground', aground

GROWS TO ME, is a natural part of my character

GUARD (n.), (i) trimming (of clothing); (ii) defence (pun, I i 148); (v.), trim (IV i 34)

HAL'D THITHER, dragged there

HALF-FAC'D, thin-faced

HALF-KIRTLES, skirts

HALLOOING, shouting (to hounds, or in battle)

HALT, limp

HAND, 'by the hand', at hand

HANGS RESOLVED CORRECTION, suspends in mid-action the resolved-upon punishment

HAPLY, perhaps

HAPPY SEASON, appropriate time

HARDLY, 'Very hardly', with great difficulty

HARK, listen; 'Hark thee hither', listen to me

HARRY TEN SHILLINGS, coins (minted under Henry VII) once worth ten shillings each, but devalued to five

HAUNCH, latter part, end

HAUTBOY, 'treble hautboy', smallest variety of oboe

HAVE AT HIM, i.e. we'll begin the contest

HEAD, army (I i 168, I iii 17, 71); 'gave his able horse the head', urged his able horse on; 'gathering head', coming to a head

HEADLAND, land at the edge of a field, left unploughed to provide access and turning-space for the ploughman

HEALTH, toast (V iii 24)

HEARKEN A' THE' END, wait and see (proverbial)

HEARSE, coffin

HEART'S ALL, i.e. thought is what counts

HEAT, 'take not the heat', do not strike while the iron is hot; 'heat is past', heavy fighting is over

HEAVINESS, sadness

HEAVY, sad (IV v 38, V ii 14, 24, 25, 26)

HECTOR, valiant leader of Trojan forces during the siege of Troy

HEED, 'take heed', be careful

HEELS, 'by the heels', i.e. by putting you in the stocks or in fetters

HEIRS OF LIFE, i.e. those who survive the executed man

HELEN, Helen of Troy (proverbial for a beautiful woman)

HELICONS, true poets inspired by the Muses (who dwelt on Mt Helicon)

HEM, (i) i.e. hiccup (II iv 30); (ii) a drinking cry (III ii 212)

HEMP-SEED, i.e. person destined for the hangman's hempen rope (and perhaps another mistake for 'homicide')

HENCE, henceforth (V v 53)

HEREFORD, Henry IV

HIE THEE, hurry

HIGH, 'high feeding', too rich food; 'high shoes . . . bunches of keys', signs of pride and self-importance

HILDING, worthless

HINCKLEY FAIR, annual fair in a market town 30 miles north-east of Stratford

HIREN, (i) 'iron' of Pistol's sword; (ii) Irene, the Greek heroine of a lost play by George Peele (pun, II iv 151, 165)

HISTORY, recount (IV i 203)

HOGSHEAD, liquor-cask

HOLD (n.), castle (Ind 35); (v.), 'holds his place', insists on his rank; 'Hold hook and line', proverbial expression from fishing meaning 'May all go well'; 'hold our safety up', maintain our safety; 'hold out', endure

HOLLAND, (i) kind of fine linen; (ii) Holland, one of the 'low countries' (pun, II ii 20)

HONEY-SEED, the Hostess's mistake for 'homicide'

HONEYSUCKLE, the Hostess's mistake for 'homicidal'

HOOK ON, stick with her

HOOK-NOS'D FELLOW, Julius Caesar (whose famous boast about an easy victory Falstaff quotes)

HORN OF ABUNDANCE, (i) cornucopia, a symbol of prosperity; (ii) cuckold's horn (said to grow on the forehead of a husband whose wife was unfaithful); (iii) horn from which lanterns were made (pun, I ii 41–2)

HOTSPUR, Harry Percy, son of the Earl of Northumberland, killed by Prince Hal ('Harry Monmouth')

HOW, how much for (III ii 36, 47)

HUMANE, secular

HUMOROUS, capricious

HUMOUR, (i) mood (II i 142, 144); (ii) disposition (II iv 226); 'humours of blood', caprices of mood; 'good humours', fine goings-on

HURLY, tumult

HUSBAND (n.), steward (V iii 11)

HUSBANDED, cultivated

HUSBANDRY, farm work (with pun on 'husband', III ii 113)

HYDRA, many-headed (Hydra was a mythological monster that grew two new heads for each one cut off)

IDLE, trifling (IV i 191); 'at idle times', i.e. when there is nothing better to do

IDLENESS, worthless foolishness

IDLY, foolishly, trivially

ILL, bad, badly

ILL-BESEEMING, evil-looking

IMAGE, symbol, representation (V ii 74, 79, 89)

IMBRUE, shed blood

IMMEDIATE FROM, heir to

IMMORTAL PART, soul

IMP, descendant of a noble family

IMPUTATION, 'with the imputation of being near their master', by implying that they are on intimate terms with their master

IN, in prison (V v 38); 'In few', in short

INCISION, i.e. a sword-wound

INDICTMENT, legal accusation

INDIFFERENCY, ordinary size

INDITED, the Hostess's mistake for 'invited'

INFER, imply

INFINITIVE, the Hostess's mistake for 'infinite'

INFLAMMATION, i.e. having our spirits aroused by drink

INNS O' COURT, the London law colleges

INSINEWED, bound by strong ties

INSTANCE, proof (III i 103, IV i 83)

INSTANT ACTION, present military action

INTELLIGENCER, messenger

INTEND, 'intends to', inclines to; 'intended in the general's name', implicit in the title of general

INTERVALLUMS, intervals (literally, the Latin legal term for vacations between court sessions)

INTREASURED, safely stored

INVEST, 'well invested', granted ample authority; 'invest Their sons with', instruct their sons in; 'invest thee with', dress yourself in

INVESTMENTS, vestments, clerical attire

INWARD (adj.), (i) civil (III i 107); (ii) sincere (IV v 148); (n.), inner organ (IV iii 102)

IRON, (i) dressed in armour; (ii) merciless (pun, IV ii 8)

IRREGULAR, lawless

ISSUE, offspring

IT ORIGINAL, its origin

JADE, nag, worn-out horse (II iv 155–6 is a misquotation from Marlowe's *Tamburlaine, Part II*)

JAPHET, 'fetch it from Japhet', trace their ancestry to Noah's son Japhet (said to be ancestor of all Europeans)

JEALOUSIES, suspicions

JERKINS, close-fitting jackets

JERUSALEM, name of a hall in Westminster Abbey

JOB, Biblical character who suffered extreme poverty with great patience

JOHN A GAUNT, Henry IV's father

JOIN'D-STOOLS, stools made by a joiner, or cabinetmaker

JORDAN, chamber-pot

JOVE, Jupiter, chief of the Roman gods; 'Jove's

case', i.e. when he transformed himself into a bull for the love of Europa

JUST, true (III ii 80, V iii 120); 'just proportion', precise number; 'just distance', halfway

JUSTLY, precisely

JUVENAL, young man

KEECH, name meaning 'lump of fat'

KEEPEST NOT RACKET, (i) aren't using your tennis racket; (ii) aren't making an uproar (pun, II ii 18)

KEN, 'within a ken', in sight

KICKSHAWS, extra delicacies

KINDLY, natural, filial

KINDREDS, clans

KIRTLE, gown

KNIGHT-ERRANT, 'she knight-errant', (i) female wandering knight; (ii) woman who 'errs' at night, i.e. prostitute (pun, V iv 23)

LACK-LINEN, shirtless, poverty-stricken

LAID UP, 'ill laid up', allowed to dry wrinkled up

LAMBKIN, a term of affection

LAND-SERVICE, military service (it would have made Falstaff immune from arrest)

LANTHORN, lantern (frequently made of horn)

LARGE, generous; 'at large', in full

LARGELY, abundantly

'LARUM BELL, alarm bell (on a watch)

LATEST, last

LAUD, praise

LAVISH, wild

LAVISHLY, wildly

LAY, lived (III ii 271)

LEATHER-COATS, rough-skinned russet apples

LEAVE (n.), permission; (v.), stop, give up (II iv 219, V v 54)

LEER UPON, glance at (rather than respectfully bowing his head, as would be expected)

LEG, 'like unto the sign of the Leg', fitting as well as the boots in a bootmaker's shop sign

LEMAN, sweetheart

LETHE, river of forgetfulness in Hades, the underworld

LETTERS, scholarship (IV i 44)

LEVEL (adj.), (i) impartial (II i 107); (ii) according (IV iv 7); (v.), take aim (III ii 258)

LEWD, loose-living

LIEF, gladly

LIEGE, lord

LIFE, 'for your life', for which you might have been hanged

LIFTING UP, dawning

LIGGENS, 'By God's liggens', an oath of unknown meaning

LIGHT, unchaste, sexually lax (II iv 284)

LIGHTEN, enlighten

LIGHTNESS, infidelity, unchastity (I ii 42)

LIKE (adj.), likely; (v.), 'liking', likening, comparing; 'like well', are in good condition

LIKELY, handsome (III ii 171)

LIMBS, i.e. men ('limbs' of the 'body of our state') (V ii 135)

LIN'D, fortified

LINEAL, rightfully inherited

LINK TO, chain for

LISPING, speaking tenderly

LIVER, considered the bodily seat of strong passions

LIVERIES, servants' uniforms (here, with royal insignia, showing them to be the King's servants)

LO, look

LOATHLY, monstrous, deformed

LODGE, harbour

LOOK, expect (I ii 39, IV ii 116); 'look you pray', see that you pray; 'look beyond', misjudge; 'look up', cheer up; 'look Too near', examine too closely (with the idea of usurping); 'Look about', look sharp!

LOOSELY STUDIED, negligent of his princely appetites

LOSING OFFICE, unprofitable job

LOW COUNTRIES, (i) low haunts, brothels; (ii) sexual part of the body; (iii) the part of Europe now occupied by Belgium, Luxemburg and the Netherlands (pun, II ii 19)

LUBBER'S HEAD, Libbard's (i.e. Leopard's) Head, a shop sign

LUCIFER'S PRIVY-KITCHEN, the devil's personal kitchen

LUMBERT STREET, Lombard Street

MADAM, i.e. the appropriate term of address for a knight's wife

MAGNANIMOUS, courageous

MAIDENHEAD, 'get a pottle-pot's maidenhead', drink a two-quart tankard of ale

MAIN CHANCE, most likely course

MAKE, 'make head', raise an army; 'make friends', gather supporters

MALLET, wooden hammer

MALMSEY-NOSE, red-nosed from drinking (malmsey was a kind of wine)

MALT-WORMS, drunkards

MAN (n.), 'man of war', soldier; 'man of this world', normal human being; (v.), 'mann'd with an agate', attended by a servant as small as a carved gemstone

MANDRAKE, root thought to resemble a man (and to be a sexual stimulant)

MAN-QUELLER, man-killer

MARE, 'whose mare's dead?', proverbial for 'what's the fuss?'; 'ride thee a nights like a mare', haunt you like a nightmare (with sexual suggestion, which Falstaff picks up)

MARK (n.), (i) the sum of thirteen shillings and four pence (two-thirds of a pound) (I ii 181, II i 29); (ii) guiding landmark (II iii 31); (v.), pay attention to, take note of

MARRIED IN CONJUNCTION, completely united

MARRY, indeed

MARSHAL'S MEN, tournament officials

MARTLEMAS, beef fattened for slaughter on Martinmas Day (11 November)

MARTYRS, 'were our royal faiths martyrs in love', even if we showed our loyalty to the King by giving our lives

MASS, 'By the mass', a mild oath

MATE, a contemptuous term of address (like 'fellow' and 'companion')

MEASUR'D, judged

MEASURE (n.), 'in some measure', to some extent

MECHANICAL, low-born, working-class

MEET, appropriate

MELTING, compassionate

MESS, small amount

METAL, (i) metal; (ii) mettle, spirit (pun, I i 116)

METE, judge

METHINKS, it seems to me

METTLE, spirit

MILE-END GREEN, military drilling-ground for London citizens

MISBECAME, did not suit

MISCARRY, come to harm or destruction

MISDOUBTS, 'As his misdoubts present occasion', of everything that attracts his suspicions

MISTAKE, misunderstand

MOCK, prove false (V ii 126)

MODEL, plan

MOE, more

MONMOUTH, 'Harry Monmouth', Prince Hal

MONSTROUS, unnatural

MORE AND LESS, men of greater and lesser rank

MORROW, morning

MOUNT, 'let desert mount', let a deserving man be promoted

MUDDY, filthy

MURD'RED, i.e. like the drone bees (not, in fact, the workers) which are killed when swarming is over

MURE, 'wrought the mure', made the wall

MUSE, am surprised

MUSTER ME ALL, all gather

MUSTERS (n.), gatherings of troops

MUTTON, (i) meat of sheep; (ii) prostitute (pun, II iv 334)

NAME, 'in an ill name', possessed of a bad reputation; 'more full of names', supplied with more men of military renown

NAVE, fat hub on the wheel of a cart (with pun on 'knave', II iv 245)

NEAF, fist

NECESSARY FORM OF THIS, inevitable operation of this principle of historical analogy

NEPTUNE, god of the sea

NEW-DATED, a few days old

NICE, (i) delicate, unmanly (I i 145); (ii) fastidiously (II iii 40); (iii) petty (IV i 191)

NIGHT-FLIES, nocturnal insects

NIGHTGOWN, dressing gown

NINE WORTHIES, proverbial group of nine great military leaders

NO SUCH MATTER, this is not at all the case

NOBLES, 'twenty nobles', just under seven pounds (the noble was a coin worth six shillings and eight pence)

NOISE (n.), band of musicians (II iv 11); (v.), 'noise abroad', spread the rumour

NOTE, bill (V i 17)

NOTICE, knowledge

NOUGHT, 'set . . . at nought', ignore, slight

NUMBER, 'By number', i.e. one hour of happiness for each tear

NUT-HOOK, slang for 'beadle' (literally, a hooked stick used in gathering nuts)

OBDURACY, stubborn impenitence

OBEDIENCE, obeisance, kneeling position (IV v 147)

OBSERVANCE, 'do observance to', i.e. kneel and beg for

OBSERVE, respect (IV iv 30, 36, 49)

OCCASION, (i) cause (I iii 5, 86); (ii) present

circumstances (IV i 72); 'As his misdoubts present occasion', of everything that attracts his suspicions

OCCUPY, have sexual relations with (the 'odious' sense)

O'ERPOSTING, 'your quiet o'erposting that action', having your offence quietly passed over

O'ERSET, defeated

OFFER, BUT NOT HOLD, threaten, but not act

OFFICE, (i) function (Ind 28, IV iv 24); (ii) duty (I i 101, II i 38–9); (iii) 'in fewer offices', with fewer rooms (I iii 47)

OLDCASTLE, Falstaff's original name (changed at the request of the descendants of the historical Sir John Oldcastle; this disclaimer is apparently directed to them)

OLIVE, olive branch (symbol of peace)

OMIT, neglect

ON'T, of it

OPENER, interpreter

OPINION, reputation

OPPOS'D DECAY, approaching ruin

OPPOSITE, 'his opposite', all its costs and difficulties; 'meeting of their opposite', encounter with their enemy

ORIENT, east

ORIGINAL, 'it original', its origin

OSTENTATION, outward display

OUCHES, (i) gems; (ii) sores, scabs (pun, II iv 48)

OUSEL, 'black ousel', blackbird (i.e. brunette, out of fashion in Elizabethan times)

OUT, drop out of the drinking (V iii 66); 'out of hand', finished

OUT-BREATH'D, out of breath

OVERLIVE, survive

OVER-RODE, outrode

OVERSCUTCH'D HUSWIFES, worn-out whores

OVERWEEN, are arrogant

OVERWHELMED, i.e. crushed to death

OWED, owned

PAGAN, prostitute

PAGE, boy or young man serving in a nobleman's retinue or at court

PAIN, effort (IV v 224)

PALLETS, 'uneasy pallets', uncomfortable straw sleeping-mats

PANTLER, servant in charge of the pantry

PAPER-FAC'D, thin- and pale-faced

PARCEL-GILT, partially gold-plated

PARCELS, details

PARLEY, meeting to discuss the terms of a truce

PART (n.), action (IV v 64); 'immortal part', soul; 'parts extremes', extremities of the body; (v.), 'part fair', part on good terms (after exchanging blows)

PART-CREATED COST, partly built object of his expense

PARTICIPATION, 'with the participation of society', by associating with one another

PARTICULAR BALLAD ELSE, ballad celebrating my personal exploits, otherwise

PARTITION, distinction

PASSING, extraordinarily

PAUL'S, St Paul's Cathedral in London (where servants sought new masters)

PAWN (n.), 'at pawn', at stake

PAWN'D, pledged

PEASCOD-TIME, early summer

PEER, nobleman

PEESEL, i.e. Pistol (the Hostess's pronunciation underscores a continuing pun on 'Pistol' and 'pizzle', penis)

PERADVENTURE, perhaps

PERCY, (i) Hotspur, son of Northumberland (I i 110, II iii 12); (ii) Northumberland (II iii 4, III i 61)

PERFECTNESS, 'in the perfectness of time', in due time

PERFORCE, of necessity

PERFUMES, the Hostess's word for 'inflames', 'pervades', and perhaps 'perfuses' (permeates)

PERIOD, conclusion

PEWTERER'S, 'with the motion of a pewterer's hammer', i.e. very quickly

PHILOSOPHER'S TWO STONES, i.e. a source of long life and great wealth (one of the legendary stones gave eternal life; the other transmuted base metals to gold)

PHYSIC, medicine

PICKING, nit-picking

PIECE, gun

PIE-CORNER, area of cooks' shops in Smithfield

PIKE, (i) long spear (with sexual suggestion) (II iv 50); (ii) variety of fish (III ii 317)

PINCH, torment

PINS, (i) wooden pegs holding together a wood-frame structure; (ii) metal pins holding together Wart's ragged clothes (pun, III ii 143)

PIPE, wind instrument

PIPPIN, variety of apple

PLACE OF DIFF'RENCE, battlefield

PLATE, metal table service (Falstaff remarks that fashionable glasses are replacing metal tankards in any case)

PLEDGE, drink to; 'pledge you a mile to th' bottom', drink to you by draining a cup a mile deep

PLUCK, pull

PLUTO'S DAMNED LAKE, Pistol's mistake for the River Styx in the underworld, of which Pluto was god (here and in what follows Pistol borrows from the ranting drama of the early 1590s)

POINT, (i) lace for tying up clothing (I i 53); (ii) lace for holding on armour (II iv 125); (iii) 'full points', full stops, periods (II iv 174); (iv) 'point of war', trumpet-call to battle (IV i 52)

POINS HIS BROTHER, Poins' brother

POLICY, craft

POLL CLAW'D, i.e. hair ruffled (by Doll)

POMFRET, Pomfret Castle, where Richard II was murdered

PORTS, gates (i.e. eyes)

POST (adv.), post-haste, with all possible speed; (n.), (i) messenger (Ind 37, I i 214, II iv 343); (ii) post-horses (IV iii 35)

POST-HORSE, horse kept at an inn to be used by travellers

POTABLE, 'med'cine potable', drug containing gold in solution, believed to preserve life and health

POTATIONS, beverages

POTION, medicine

POTTLE-POT, two-quart tankard; 'get a pottle-pot's maidenhead', i.e. drink a two-quart tankard of ale

POWER, army

POX, venereal disease; 'A pox of', a curse on

PRACTIS'D UPON, deceived

PRAWNS, shrimp

PRAY, ask, I ask

PRECEPTS, legal writs, warrants

PRECISE, scrupulously

PRECISELY, thoroughly

PREGNANCY, quick-wittedness, intelligence

PRENTICE, apprentice (as a drawer would normally be)

PRESENT, immediate

PRESENTED, represented

PRESENTLY, immediately

PRESERVE THEE, i.e. from moral corruption (the coin was stamped with a cross)

PRE-SURMISE, foreknowledge, presentiment

PRIAM, King of Troy

PRICE, great value

PRICK, mark or write down on a list of names; (i) on Satan's list of the damned (II iv 320); (ii) with puns on other meanings, as follows: 'worried', 'turned sour' (i.e. 'mouldy'), and 'posessed of a penis' (III ii 111); 'pin' (III ii 143); 'dress' (III ii 151); 'poke with a stick in bull-baiting' (III ii 171, 174)

PRIVY-KITCHEN, personal kitchen

PRODIGAL, Prodigal Son of Christ's parable (Luke xv, 11–32)

PROFACE, polite dinner welcome (from the French for 'may it do you good')

PROFITED, i.e. by his companionship with Falstaff

PROJECT, 'in project of a power', anticipating an army, which turned out in fact to be

PROOF, 'come to any proof', turn out well

PROPER, (i) belonging to (I iii 32); (ii) own (V ii 109); 'proper fellow of my hands', i.e. a good fighter and a good thief

PROPORTION, 'the just proportion', the exact number

PROPOSE, imagine

PROVIDED, prepared (II iii 50)

PSALMIST, 'as the Psalmist saith', i.e. in Psalm lxxxix, 48)

PUFF, slang for 'cowardly braggart' (thus Pistol takes Shallow's comparison as an insult to Falstaff)

PUISSANCE, strength

PULSIDGE, the Hostess's mistake for 'pulse'

PURCHAS'D, acquired rather than inherited (a legal term)

PUT, 'put forth', wager; 'put him to', enlist him as

QUAFF'D, 'tyranny, which never quaff'd but blood', i.e. even a tyrant who drank nothing but blood

QUALITY, rank (IV i 11, V v 70)

QUANTITIES, little pieces

QUARREL IN PARTICULAR, particular reason for complaint

QUEAN, hussy, bad-mannered woman

QUESTION, 'in question', under suspicion

QUIT, (i) forgiven; (ii) repaid (pun on (i) and (ii), II iv 330); (iii) free of debt (III i 232)

QUITTANCE, 'faint quittance', feeble resistance

QUIVER, nimble

QUOIT (v.), throw

QUOITS (n.), game in which rings are tossed at a stake

QUOTH-A, said he

RAGE, lust (IV iv 63)

RAIN UPON REMEMBRANCE, water with tears the symbol of remembrance, rosemary

RAMPALLIAN, scoundrel

RANK, (i) foul (III i 39); (ii) bloated, swollen (IV i 64)

RASCAL, (i) scoundrel; (ii) lean deer (puns, II iv 41, V iv 30)

RASCAL-YEA-FORSOOTH KNAVE, a scoundrelly Puritan tradesman whose strongest oath is 'Yea, forsooth'

RASH, violent

RATE (n.), estimated number; (v.), (i) calculate (I iii 44); (ii) scold (III i 68, V ii 70)

RATSBANE, poison

RAZE OUT, erase

REASON WILL, reason suggests that

RECKONINGS, tavern bills

RECORDATION, a memorial

RECREANT, traitorous and cowardly

RED LATTICE, tavern window (the lattices of which were often painted 'red)

RED WHEAT, reddish variety of wheat sown in late August

REMEMBRANCE, reminder (V ii 115)

REMEMB'RED, mentioned (V ii 142)

REMISSION, 'ragged and forestall'd remission', beggarly pardon offered on terms I could not accept

REND'RED, announced (IV ii 87)

RESCUE, taking persons out of legal custody by force (legal term)

RESPECT, consideration; 'in respect of poverty', i.e. because he is too poor to pay the fine; 'with good respect', with proper ceremony (ironical)

RETAIL, repeat

RETREAT IS MADE, the order for retreat has been given

REVOLUTION OF THE TIMES, alterations brought by time

RHEUMATIC, cold and wet humour (bodily fluid believed to control temperament) – the Hostess's mistake for 'choleric', the hot and dry humour

RIDES THE WILD MARE, plays a game in which boys line up as the 'mare', and other boys leap on top as 'riders'

RIGHT FENCING GRACE, proper form in fencing

RIGOL, circle

RINGING IN, ringing the church bells to celebrate

RIOT, (i) wild living, moral laxity (IV iv 62, IV v 136, V v 63); (ii) civil disorder (IV v 135)

RIPE (v.), make ripe

ROAD, i.e. prostitute (used by all who pass her way)

ROAD-WAY, i.e. beaten path

ROBIN HOOD, 'And Robin Hood, Scarlet, and John', line from a ballad

RODS, punishments

ROOD, cross

ROUNDLY, plainly, thoroughly

ROUSED, raised

ROUT, mob

ROWEL-HEAD, spiked metal wheel of a spur

RUDE, harsh, violent

RUFF, large pleated collar; 'murder your ruff', tear your collar

RUSHES, spread on the floor or street for ceremonial occasions

SACK, Spanish white wine

SACKCLOTH, 'ashes and sackcloth', traditional Biblical apparel for mourning and penance

SAD, serious (V i 76)

SADLY, soberly

SAGE, wise

SAINT GEORGE'S FIELD, London park

SALTNESS, aged flavour (like that of preserved meat)

SAMINGO, Sir Mingo (hero of this drinking song)

SANCTIFIED, i.e. on a crusade to the Holy Land

SANCTITIES, saints

SATURN AND VENUS, the old patriarch of the gods and the goddess of love (the two planets were believed never to appear 'in conjunction')

SAVING, no offence to

SCAB, (i) rascal; (ii) wart (pun, III ii 267)

SCALD'ST WITH SAFETY, burns while it protects

SCAPE, escape

SCHEDULE, scroll of paper

SCHOOL OF TONGUES, multitude of voices or languages (i.e. since his obesity says who he is)

SCOGGIN, name meaning 'buffoon, jester'

SCORE, tavern account (II i 23)

SCRUPLE, (i) doubt; (ii) a small weight used to

measure doses of medicine (pun, I ii 123–4)

SCULLION, kitchen-maid of the most menial rank

SCURVY, wretched, miserable

SEA-COAL, coal (as opposed to charcoal)

SEAL, 'seal with him', (i) come to an agreement with him; (ii) mold him to my purposes (pun, IV iii 128); 'seal'd up', confirmed

SEARCHING, searching out weak points, i.e. potent

SECOND BODY, representative

SECOND BROTHER, i.e. one who receives no inheritance

SECT, sex

SEE (n.), diocese

SEEMING (n.), outward appearance

SEMBLABLE COHERENCE, striking similarity

'SEMPER IDEM' FOR 'OBSQUE HOC NIHIL EST', 'always the same' for 'without this [i.e. seeing the King?] there is nothing' (two Latin mottoes)

SENSIBLE, (i) reasonable; (ii) feeling pain (pun, I ii 183)

SERVICE, (i) military service; (ii) farm work; (iii) sexual potency (pun, III ii 244)

SET, 'set on to this', put up to this (by someone else); 'set off', ignored; 'sets it in act', puts it to work (with pun on the 'Act', the name for the Oxford degree-granting ceremony)

SEVEN STARS, 'we have seen the seven stars', i.e. I have had to sleep outdoors before ('the seven stars' are either the Pleiades, or the Great Bear/Big Dipper)

SEVERAL, separate

SEVERALLY, separately

SHADOW, (i) shade from the sun; (ii) likeness, image; (iii) fictitious name written in the 'muster-book' for which the captain could draw pay (puns, III ii 120–134)

SHALLOWLY, without consideration

SHERRIS, SHERRIS-SACK, sherry (or a strong white wine resembling it)

SHIFT (n.), 'make other shift', manage some other way; 'made a shift', (i) found a way; (ii) made a shirt; (iii) caused a change of clothes (pun, II ii 19–20); (v.), 'shift me', change my clothes

SHOOT, 'shot a fine shoot', was a fine shot with a bow and arrow

SHOVE-GROAT SHILLING, coin shoved along a smooth board in a game resembling shuffleboard

SHOW, look (II ii 5, IV i 63, IV ii 4, IV iii 47, 50); 'show vilely', look shameful

SHREWD, nasty, vicious

SHREWS, nagging, scolding women

SHRIEVE, sheriff

SHROVE-TIDE, period of feasting before Lent

SI FORTUNE ME TORMENTE SPERATO ME CONTENTO, if Fortune torments me, hope contents me (garbled Spanish/Italian proverb, repeated in a different form at V v 97)

SICK, i.e. sick with longing (V iii 133)

SIGNIORIES, estates

SINGLE, feeble

SIRRAH, term of address used to inferiors (or to oneself, at V iii 15)

SISTERS THREE, the mythological Fates (of whom Atropos was one) who spun, drew out and cut life's thread

SLIPPERY, sliding rapidly past

SLOPS, wide trousers

SMALL BEER, beer thinned with water

SMELL A FOX, be suspicious (as the Lord Chief Justice is)

SMITHFIELD, London market

SMOOTH-PATES, Puritan tradesmen, who wore their hair cut short

SNEAP, rebuke

SOFT, gently (V ii 97)

SOIL OF THE ACHIEVEMENT, moral stain of its acquisition (with pun on the meaning 'earth')

SOMETHING, somewhat; 'something a', a somewhat

SOMEWHAT, i.e. a feat or two in drinking

SOON AT NIGHT, early this evening

SORE, very

SORTANCE, 'hold sortance with his quality', accord with his rank

SORTED, 'ill sorted', in bad company

SOUND, (i) resound, echo (I iii 74); (ii) 'sound the bottom', measure the depth (i.e. guess the nature) (IV ii 51); (iii) speak (V ii 119)

SOUTH, south wind (thought to bring storms) (II iv 350)

SPEAK . . . FAIR, address with courtesy and respect

SPEAKER, intermediary between the members of Parliament and the King (i.e. between men and God)

SPENT, (i) consumed, eaten; (ii) killed; (iii) sexually impotent (puns, III ii 117–118)

SPIRIT, intuition (I i 92)

SPIT WHITE, probably, a sign of heavy drinking

SPREAD, lay the tablecloth

SPRING, 'in the spring of day', at daybreak

SPURN AT, mock, reject contemptuously

STAMFORD, site in Lincolnshire of famous horse and cattle fairs

STAND, act as (III ii 215, 224, IV iii 81); 'stand upon', (i) insist on having (I ii 34, IV i 165); (ii) depend on (III ii 143); 'stand to't', stand up in the face of danger; 'stand up to me', stand up for me; 'stand the push', tolerate the impudence

STATE, (i) grandeur (III i 13); (ii) state of affairs (IV i 115); (iii) dignity (IV v 121); (iv) royal office (IV v 213, V ii 99); (v) men of high rank (V ii 142)

STAVES, (i) 'armed staves in charge', steel-tipped lances in position for the charge (IV i 120); (ii) staffs, walking-sticks (V i 61)

STAY, (i) wait, await (I i 48, II iv 359, IV v 81, 94, 99); (ii) keep (IV i 123); (iii) stop (IV iii 71)

STEW'D PRUNES, associated with the 'stews', or brothels

STEWS, brothels (Falstaff alludes to a proverb advising against getting a servant in St Paul's, a horse at Smithfield, or a wife in Westminster)

STICK, hesitate (I ii 18)

STIFF-BORNE, obstinately pursued

STILL, continually, always

STILL-STAND, 'makes a still-stand', stands still

STOCKFISH, name meaning 'dried cod'

STOMACH, (i) courage (I i 129); (ii) appetite (IV iv 105, 107)

STOP (n.), 'of so easy and so plain a stop', may be played so easily; (v.), (i) block up (Ind 1, I i 79, IV i 65); (ii) fill (I i 78, I ii 39)

STORE, 'good store', a great quantity

STRAIGHT, immediately

STRAIN (n.), strong feeling

STRAINED, excessive

STRAND, shore

STRANGE, (i) reluctant (I i 94); (ii) foreign (IV iv 69)

STRANGE-ACHIEVED, hard-earned

STRANGELY, distantly, as if I were a stranger

STRATAGEM, (i) violent act (I i 8); (ii) trick (II iv 20)

STRAY, stragglers

STRIKE SAIL, lower their sails; i.e. submit themselves

STUFF, cloth (II iv 264)

SUBORN'D TO GRATE ON YOU, induce to harass you

SUBSTANCE, 'but much of the father's substance', i.e. this son doesn't contain very much of the father's substance

SUBSTITUTE (n.), i.e. the King (who was believed to be God's deputy on earth)

SUBSTITUTED, sent in the King's name

SUCCESS, successions

SUCCESSIVELY, as an inherited right

SUFFER, permit; 'suffering flesh to be eaten', (i) allowing meat to be eaten (during Lent and fast days); (ii) keeping a brothel (pun, II iv 331)

SUFFERANCE, suffering

SUFFICIENT, able-bodied

SUGGESTION, suspicion, false insinuation

SULLEN, mournful

SUPERFLUITY, 'one for superfluity', an extra one

SUPPLY, SUPPLIES, reinforcements

SURETY, 'a double surety', both bodily and spiritual allegiance

SURFEITED, grown tired (of Henry)

SURFEITING, gluttonous

SURFEIT-SWELL'D, swollen with excessive food and drink

SUSPIRE, breathe

SWAGGER, bully, bluster

SWAY ON, advance

SWEAT, (i) perspiration; (ii) plague or venereal disease (pun, Epil 28)

SWIMS AGAINST YOUR STREAM OF QUALITY, goes against the inclination of your disposition and rank

SWING'D, thrashed

SWINGE-BUCKLERS, swashbucklers, ruffians

TABLES, notebook

TAKE, 'take not the heat', do not strike while the iron is hot; 'take not on me', do not present myself; 'ta'en up', enlisted

TAKING-UP, 'is through with them in honest taking-up', has completed an honest deal with them

TALL, (i) valiant (III ii 60); (ii) tall in height (pun on (i) and (ii), V i 57)

TALLOW, animal fat (referring to Falstaff's obesity)

TAPSTER, waiter in a tavern

TARRY DINNER, stay long enough to eat dinner

TASTE, test (II iii 52)

TELL, 'cannot tell', (i) do not know; (ii) will not be counted as good money (pun, I ii 157)

TEMPER (n.), character

TEMPERALITY, the Hostess's combination of 'temper' and 'quality'

TEMP'RING, softening with warmth, like sealing-wax

TENNIS-COURT-KEEPER KNOWS, i.e. because whenever Poins has a shirt to wear and another to change into, he'll be on the court

TENOUR OF OUR WORD, our stated intention

TERMS, court sessions ('four terms' make up a legal year) (V i 75)

TESTER, sixpence

TEWKESBURY MUSTARD, excellent mustard (famous for sharpness, however, not thickness)

THEME, affair

THEREAFTER AS THEY BE, it depends on their quality

THEWS, sinews, bodily strength

THICK, (i) rapidly, impetuously (II iii 24); (ii) dull (III ii 302); (iii) fat (pun on (ii) and (iii), IV iii 57)

THIEF, wretch (used affectionately)

THOUGHTFUL, careful

THOUSANDS, i.e. thousands of lice

THROAT, 'in my (your) throat', outrageously

TIDY, plump

TILLY-FALLY, nonsense, fiddlesticks

TILTYARD, ground set aside for jousts and other sports

TIRING, 'come tiring on', ride on in exhaustion

TIRRITS, apparently the Hostess's combination of 'terrors' and 'fits'

TISICK, name derived from 'phthisic', a consumptive cough

TITLE-LEAF, title-page (describing a book's contents)

TO BROTHER BORN AN HOUSEHOLD CRUELTY, line absent from some texts and never satisfactorily explained; Henry IV had executed the Archbishop's brother

TOLLING, gathering (IV v 75)

TO-NIGHT, last night (II ii 161)

TOSS . . . IN A BLANKET, a form of punishment and humiliation

TOUCH GROUND, i.e. like a ship hitting rocks

TOWARD, 'goodly stuff toward', fine things about to happen

TRADE, 'lift him where most trade of danger ranged', carry him to the most dangerous areas of battle

TRAIN, (i) army (IV ii 93); (ii) retinue, attendants (V v 4 SD, 73 SD)

TRANSLATE, transform

TRAVEL-TAINTED, exhausted by travel

TRAVERSE, shift gun's position so as to take aim

TRIGON, 'fiery Trigon', on the four divisions of the zodiac, containing the 'fiery' signs of Aries, Leo, and Sagittarius (i.e. Bardolph's red face)

TRIMM'D, dressed

TRIPE-VISAG'D, with a pale and pockmarked face

TROIANT, Trojan

TROTH, 'by my troth', indeed

TRULY, faithfully

TRUNCHEON, beat with a club

TRY, test, put to the test

TURK'S TRIBUTE, annual tribute-money demanded by the Sultan of Turkey

TURNBULL STREET, notorious haunt of thieves and prostitutes

TURN'D ON THEMSELVES, (i) bent, like swords made of soft lead; (ii) fled from the battle (pun, I i 118)

TWICE AND ONCE, i.e. a time or two

UNCOUNTED, innumerable

UNDO, ruin; 'undone by his going', bankrupted by his going to war with his bill unpaid

UNEQUAL, unjust

UNFATHER'D HEIRS, unnaturally begotten children (fathered by demons)

UNFIRM, weak

UNPICKED, unenjoyed

UNSEASONED, unseasonable, late

UP, up in arms (I i 189)

UP-SWARM'D THEM, raised them in swarms

USE, (i) treat, behave toward (II ii 124, 129, V i 29–30); (ii) 'use the person', act in the character (V ii 73); (iii) 'us'd', been accustomed (V ii 114)

UTIS, 'old utis', a fine time, lots of fun ('utis' is both a dialectal word for 'noise, confusion', and a word for 'festival')

UTMOST MAN OF EXPECTATION, all the soldiers we can expect

VAIL, 'Gan vail his stomach', began to fail in courage

VAIN, foolish

VALUATION, 'our valuation', the King's estimation of us

VANITY, frivolity, foolishness

VANTAGE, favourable position, superiority; 'vantage of ground', standing-place on higher ground

VARLET, (i) scoundrel (II i 42); (ii) servant (V iii 12)

VASSAL, peasant

VAWARD, vanguard

VENTURE, (i) attempt (Epil 6); (ii) business venture, trading voyage (Epil 9); 'at a venture', recklessly; 'venture of Bordeaux stuff', cargo of Bordeaux wine

VICE, (i) grip (II i 21); (ii) 'Vice's dagger', this wooden dagger wielded by the Vice, a character in morality plays (III ii 307)

VICT'LERS, victuallers, tavernkeepers

VIRTUE, 'In very ample virtue', with full authority

VISITATION, violent buffeting

VITAL COMMONERS AND INLAND PETTY SPIRITS, vital spirits believed to be contained by the blood

VIZ., namely

VULGAR HEART, feelings of the common people

WAGS (n.), jokers, lively fellows (as well as being young)

WANT, lack

WANTON, (i) trifling, effeminate (I i 148); (ii) self-indulgent (IV i 55); (iii) frivolous (IV i 191)

WARDER, staff used as a signal by one presiding over a formal combat

WARRANT, assure

WASSAIL CANDLE, large candle designed to burn all night, used at feasts

WASTE, (i) obliterate (IV v 216); (ii) use up, consume (IV i 215, IV v 217)

WATCH-CASE, either (i) sentry-box; or (ii) case containing a constantly ticking watch; or (iii) a pun on both meanings

WATCHWORD, rallying cry

WATER, urine

WATER-WORK, water-colour

WAX, (i) beeswax; (ii) to grow (pun followed up in 'growth', I ii 1)

WEAKER VESSEL, Biblical term for the female sex

WEIGH WITH, match (in foolishness)

WELKIN, sky

WELL SAID, well done (III ii 267, V iii 6)

WELL-APPOINTED, well-equipped

WEN, swelling, tumour

WHEESON, Whitsun (Pentecost)

'WHEN ARTHUR FIRST IN COURT', first line of a ballad, 'Sir Launcelot du Lake'

'WHERE IS THE LIFE THAT LATE I LED', line from a lost ballad

WHEREBY, whereupon (II i 91–2)

WHEREUPON, why (II iv 85)

WHIPPING-CHEER, the hospitality of the whip (whipping was the usual punishment for prostitutes)

WHORESON, miserable, abominable

WILD, i.e. taking my youthful wildness with him (V ii 123)

WILLS, desires

WINKING, shutting his eyes

WINNOW'D, dropped in the wind to separate the chaff from the grain

WIT, intelligence

WITHAL, (i) with (I ii 116, IV ii 95); (ii) in addition (V iii 132)

WITNESS'D USURPATION, evidence of encroachment

WOMB, belly (IV iii 19)

WONTED, customary

WORD, Holy Scripture (IV ii 10); 'I have spoke at a word', I mean what I say

WORKING, (i) perception (IV ii 22); (ii) exertion (IV iv 41); (iii) efforts (IV v 207)

WOT, wilt; 'wot ta', wilt thou

WRESTED, twisted

WRIT MAN, called himself a man

WRONGS, bad news

WROUGHT OUT LIFE, came through alive

YEOMAN, constable's assistant

ZEAL, (i) religious devotion (II iv 316; with pun on 'seal', IV ii 27); (ii) eagerness (V v 13)